I0065019

PUBLISHER

İMMİB

İMMİB
(İstanbul Mineral and Metals
Exporters' Association)
REPRESENTATIVE OF THE PUBLISHER
S. Armağan VURDU, on behalf of İMMİB
HEADQUARTERS / MANAGEMENT
DIŞ TİCARET KOMPLEKSİ - A BLOK
Çobançeşme Mevkii, Sanayi Cad. 34197
Yenibosna - Bahçelievler/ İstanbul Turkey
Tel: +90 212 454 00 00 Fax: +90 212 454 00 01
www.immib.org.tr immib@immib.org.tr
BOARD OF PUBLISHING
**Tahsin ÖZTİRYAKİ, Rıdvan MERTÖZ,
Murat AKYÜZ, Fatih Kemal EBİÇLİOĞLU,
İsmail ERDOĞAN, Fatih ÖZER,
Ümit KOŞKAN, Muharrem KAYILI, Murat
TUNCEL, İrem UZUNÖZ, Buğra EROL,
Merve TAŞDEMİR**

PUBLISHING TEAM
DÜNYA
ajansd
MANAGING EDITOR
Gürhan DEMİRBAŞ
ASSISTANT MANAGING EDITOR
Eser SOYGÜDER YILDIZ
ART DIRECTOR
Hakan KAHVECİ
NEWS EDITOR
Mehtap GÖRAL
GRAPHIC DESIGN
Şahin BİNGÖL
PHOTOGRAPHERS
Eren AKTAŞ
CONTACT NUMBER
Tel: 0212 440 27 63 - 0212 440 29 68
ajansd@dunya.com
www.ajansdyayincilik.com
CORPORATE SALES MANAGER
Özlem ADAŞ
(0212) 0212 440 27 65
ADVERTISEMENT BOOKING
Nazlı DEMİREL
(0212) 440 27 69
nazli.demirel@dunya.com
PRINTED AT
İstanbul Basım Promosyon
Basın Ekspres Yolu Cemal Ulusoy Cad.
No:38/A 34620, Sefaköy-İstanbul
info@istanbulprinting.com
Tel: 0212 603 26 20
TRANSLATION
UNIVERSAL DİL HİZM. VE YAY. LTD. ŞTİ
(0212) 212 02 40
www.universaldil.com.tr

PUBLISHING DATE AND PLACE
İstanbul, Winter 2016

TYPE OF PUBLICATION *International Periodical
Kitchenware Turkish is published 4 times a year by Ajans D.
In whole or in part of any material in this publication without
prior written permission from Ajans D is expressly prohibited.
The written materials are the sole responsibility of each of the
writers, and the advertisements published in the magazine are
the sole responsibility of each advertiser.
A complimentary copy from İMMİB. ISSN-1309-4998*

kitchen ware

edito

Hello,

We are thrilled to meet with you at the Ambiente 2016 fair, the world's largest fair in the kitchen and housewares sector, in which İMMİB will attend with 71 firms with a national participation for the 21st time this year.

Let us begin with a brief news tour… We have organized a sectoral trade delegation visit to Fort Lauderdale/USA between October 25-29, 2015 with the attendance of 9 firms from the Turkish house and kitchenwares sector. Each company had an average of 30 meetings during the two day bilateral business meetings event.

23 firms included in the 2nd Turkish House and Kitchen Wares Overseas Marketing Team that is conducted in partnership between Istanbul Ferrous & Non-Ferrous Metals Exporters' Association (İDDMİB), and ZÜCDER (Turkish Glassware Association) were visited by consultants, and a needs analysis was carried out. With this needs analysis, the cluster's consulting needs, strategy, and target markets were determined. The training events specified in the need analysis will be followed with local and overseas marketing events.

The sector showed great interest in the Industrial Kitchen UR-GE project that had been announced during the past months, and that will be conducted by İDDMİB and TÜSİD (Laundry and Catering Equipment Manufacturers' and Distributors' Association) in partnership, and 48 companies participated in the project. The first stage of the project, needs analysis, will be carried out in January and February and the cluster will begin operations expeditiously.

We have organized the second instance of the Plastic and Metal Packaging Design Competition, for the purpose of offering export products to world markets with original and innovative packaging designs. In addition to cash prizes, winners who ranked first in the competition also earned the chance to visit prestigious packaging fairs overseas, and to use the Ministry of Finance's overseas education scholarship.

Let us briefly mention the other titles we have included in our magazine, which we hope you will read with pleasure. In our brand story page, we hosted Jumbo. Ege, Eminem, Göreme, Kavsan, Öztiryakiler, Porland, Renga, SNT were other firms with which we made interviews. In our styling pages, we aimed to present you with the designs the Turkish kitchenware sector prepared for 2016 and for the Ambiente Fair. We believe that these star products of Turkish firms will interest you as well.

On our nostalgia page, we discussed the properties of tinsmithing, which dates back to 3000 B.C. and is known as part of the Turkish culture. In this issue, we heard the design stories of four designers who have made their mark with successful products in the kitchenwares sector, Sevin Coşkun, Burcu Büyükünal, Meriç Kara, and Seyman Çay.

We conversed with experienced chef Mehmet Siriş about the profession of cooking said that his experience in Çırağan Palace Hotel Kempinski Istanbul which lasted for nearly a decade had set the roadmap of his life, and we heard his delicious recipes.

In hopes of meeting you at the IHHS and Hong Kong fairs in the days to come…

Chairman of Istanbul Ferrous and Non-Ferrous Metals Exporters' Association **Rıdvan Mertöz**
Chairman of Istanbul Chemicals and Chemical Products Exporters' Association **Murat Akyüz**
Chairman of Electrical, Electronics and Services Exporters' Association **Fatih Kemal Ebiçlioğlu**

CONTENTS

turkish **kitchen**ware

ozti

professional kitchen equipment

öztiryakiler

www.oztiryakiler.com.tr

LATEST NEWS FROM KITCHENWARE SECTOR

AŞK-I OSMANİ

Doyenne of Ottoman Art History Professor Nurhan Atasoy, PhD, and architect-art historian and novelist Professor Gül İrepoğlu, PhD have combined their wealth of knowledge in a peerless creation. Implemented by Bernardo, the masters of table design, the Aşk-ı Osmani collection inspired by Ottoman patterns and Ottoman colors, carry the beauty of the past to our day with a new approach. As the Zerre-i Kubbe, Kısmet-i Kubbe, Bereket-i Kubbe, İkrami, Altın Kafes, Levni, Gül-i Firuze, and Çintemani series were created on the inspiration of traditional Ottoman patterns, the product and pattern design-application was the work of the skilled hands of Sevil Acar. The Bernardo Aşk-ı Osmani Collection which is based on knowledge filled inspirations from Ottoman art, and is made up of pieces that will be used with pleasure in experiencing the gusto of the palace at homes, includes varied products such as dining sets, tea and Turkish coffee cup sets, trays, bowls, platters, service pieces, chandeliers, gondolas, pans, Turkish delight serving dishes, fruit bowls, and appetizer bowls.
www.bernardo.com.tr

COMPLIANT WITH EUROPEAN STANDARDS

The Artenova AE 780 T kitchen sink model was offered for use with a modern and striking design. The product dimensions are 480 x 780 x 170. It can be manufactured as 0.60 mm and 0.80 mm at the ideal thickness desired. The product also comes with satin and decorated surface finishes. Our product which has two different designs can be manufactured with overflow from the tub or drain board. Since a siphon outlet can be used with a small or large whole, it is suitable for use with garbage compactor. AISI 304 18/10 cr.ni stainless steel compliant with European standards is used in the production of Artenova branded kitchen sinks. Therefore the products are offered with an indefinite company guarantee.
www.artenova.com.tr

THE COOKPLUS TEA MAKER AND KITCHEN SET

The tea you steep with the Cookplus Tea Maker maintains its freshness for a long time. It does not lose its flavor after the third glass, like tea does when it is steeped in a regular teapot. It is suitable for nuclear and crowded families in terms of capacity. The glass upper section highlights the clarity of the tea. The kitchen set will charm you with its color and what it does. You can recommend to your loved ones with ease.
www.cookplus.com

ARZUM FIRRIN

Thanks to Arzum's award winning side feed toaster design "Fırrın" which is the first of its kind in the world, you can toast foods of all sizes ranging from pitahs to beureks, bagels, and buns.

"Arzum Fırrın", the award winning product of Arzum which creates big differences with small touches is becoming a fixture in your kitchen for its decorative design and convenience of use. Having won the IF Design, Design Turkey, Plus X Award, and the Hong Kong Industry Award, Fırrın sets itself apart by being the first side feeding toaster in the world. Arzum Fırrın which defrosts bread taken off the freezer within minutes thanks to its defrosting function can be easily cleaned thanks to its removable sliding oven tray.
www.arzum.com.tr

MINI BOX

MIDI BOX

MAXI BOX

Ay·kasa ®
Folding Crates

www.aykasa.com.tr   info@aykasa.com.tr

We are looking for country distributors

LATEST NEWS FROM KITCHENWARE SECTOR

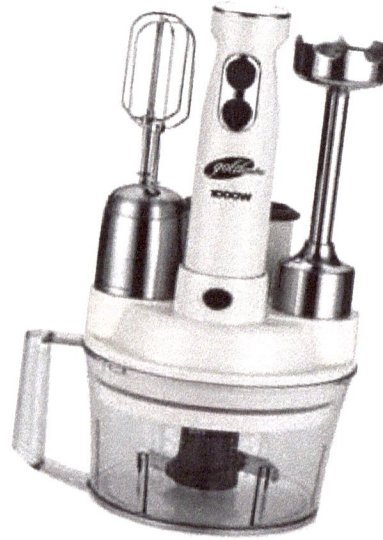

THE SILENT CHEF IN THE KITCHEN

GoldMaster's food processor which began production in Turkey, offering technology and design with a unique harmony, the Elena Max becomes the greatest helper of people who enter the kitchen. Having served with a power of production and R&D at global standards for 40 years, GoldMaster turns food preparation into entertainment with the Elena Max food processor it began manufacturing at its factory in Turkey. Elena Max which serves the functions of chopping, blending, mixing, slicing, and grating in the easiest and fastest way thanks to its powerful 1000 W high performance motor, sets itself apart from its competitors in the market for its silent operation.

www.goldmaster.com.tr

TO ENJOY POPCORN

Esse has prepared a special popcorn series for people who delight in watching movies or TV series at home during long winter nights. Popcorn pots specially designed for a fresh and warm treat to be enjoyed in front of the TV, the Essenso Zippy and Whirley await film enthusiasts planning to spend evenings at home, at Esse stores.

Zippy which is very convenient and clean thanks to its aluminum frame and non-stick interior surface, Zippy guarantees the same deliciousness down to the last kernel of corn, thanks to its patented stirring mechanism. Hassle-free popcorn can be enjoyed at any kitchen with a glass lid that allows viewing the inside of the pot during the popping process, and a silicone lidded hole that makes adding ingredients a breeze. The recipe booklet that comes with Essenso Zippy guides those who wish to sample different popcorn flavors. Essenso Zippy is also convenient in that it can be washed in the dishwasher.

www.esse.com.tr

Ahmetal Pots & Pans Baskets

AHMETAL USES LATEST TECHNOLOGIES

Ahmetal located in Bolvadin-Afyon-Turkey, produces baskets for all kind of pots and pans, exporting 30% of production overseas (France, Belgium, Spain, Egypt, Lebanon etc.), and 70% of its production to local markets while seeking strong customers and trying to extend market shares. Ahmetal carries out all of these activities in a 3000 square meter factory with a staff of 25 , using state of the art technologies and high quality raw materials that are not harmful to the end user or the environment. Tin coated baskets for pots and pans.

www.ahmetal.com.tr

LunArt Enamel
Kitchenware & Service Products

LA LunArt ®
"Enamel"
Made In TURKEY
by LUYANO

The "LunArt Enamel" collection which is produced in Turkey, combines aesthetics and enjoyment for outstanding cuisines. Also,you can make colorful presentations with enamel tabletops by Lunart Enamel.

Luyano Ltd. is the only company who sells its unique enamel collections in Turkey and all over the World.

Enamel Collections can be customized with tailor made models and with special colors upon request.

LunArt by Luyano
Company Name ; LUYANO Zücaciye Tekstil San.ve Tic.Ltd.Şti.
Istanbul- TURKEY / e.mail ; info@luyano.com.tr / https:// www. luyano.com.tr

LATEST NEWS FROM KITCHENWARE SECTOR •

INNOVATIONS FROM VESTEL

The Vestel Brunch Series 2000 Inox Red Water Heater will complement your breakfasts. Having a large capacity of 1.8 liters, the water heater allows longer use thanks to its Inox main body. While its stainless steel hidden resistance allows healthy and elegant use, its washable calc filter makes your life easy. Fresh fruit and vegetable juices you will prepare with Vestel's Mix & Go Blender series will add freshness and health to your breakfasts in the new year. Its easily removed and remounted stainless blades allow you to prepare healthy beverages from all types of fruits and vegetables. You can carry your health-filled beverages anywhere with their mixing bottles offered in two sizes.
www.vestel.com.tr

FRIMA VARIOCOOKING CENTER MULTIFICIENCY®

İnoksan which has embraced the principle of always offering the most advanced technology to its customers has brought the VarioCooking Center MULTIFICIENCY® that has become indispensable to expert chefs in thousands of professional kitchens around the world to enterprises in Turkey.
The VarioCooking Center MULTIFICIENCY® has expedited the trend of multifunctionality in kitchen technology by combining all functions including roasting, boiling, frying, grilling, slow cooking, pressure cooking and Sous-Vide cooking in a single device.
With 4 times the speed and 40% less energy consumption as compared to conventional cooking methods the VarioCooking Center MULTIFICIENCY® offers economy of time and energy, the greatest need of professional kitchens in today's world. The economy of space in the professional kitchen which is made possible by using a single device for many functions is a unique solution for every shrinking spaces and it creates a lean working environment for the user.
www.inoksan.com

SOFT GRANITE SERIES

Savasan Enamelware has been in this sector for over 40 years and increased its reputation each and every year. Thanks to our R&D department, we have revolutionized cookware. Not only the shape but also the materials used in production must meet the expectations of the end-user. The Soft Granit Series was born of countless researches. It is heavy gauge & weight, just like granite stone. With the best nonstick finish, it is easily cleaned and saves precious time.
www.savasan.com

rengA ®

new collection 2016

AMBIENTE 12 - 16 February 2016
HALL: 6.1 STAND: D10
FRANKFURT, GERMANY

IDEAL HOME HOUSEWARE 31 March- 3 April 2016
HALL:2 STAND: C01
ISTANBUL, TURKEY

HONG KONG HOUSEWARE EX. 20 - 23 April 2016
HALL: 3F STAND: F03
HONG KONG

ZUCHEX FAIR 22-25 September 2016
HALL:2 STAND C01
ISTANBUL ,TURKEY

MEGA SHOW HONG KONG 20-23 October 2016
HONG KONG

facebook.com/rengasosyal
twitter.com/rengasosyal
instagram.com/rengasosyal

www.renga.com.tr

mercanlar

LATEST NEWS FROM KITCHENWARE SECTOR

COOK IN STYLE

Instead of common application on aluminium in the world market, Eternity shows its difference once again by using healthy porcelain enameled steel as a substrate for its unique production process. Whereas innovative 4 layer coating presents a healthier surface for cooking, it also provides a perfect functioning performance. As a result, the combination the of latest coating technology and natural inspiration elevate cookto a higher professional level. With a variety of styles and sizes, you'll be sure to find a Granite Cooking Utensil that's just right for you.
www.guzelis.com.tr

AYKASA FOLDING CRATES

Aykasa folding crates are designed for practical houseware usage with space saving advantage. There are different sizes of Aykasa folding crates with volume capacities starting from 4 liters to 45 liters.
When you need to use the folding crates, you just open easily. When you don't need to use the folding crates, you can easily fold and put them in any storage area in the kitchen, they take very small space. All Aykasa folding crates are made by the same material that is for baby bottles, conforming to Food Codex. Aykasa folding crates have maximum air circulation design, so you can put your fruits and vegetables inside to keep them more fresh. Aykasa folding crates are durable in deep freezer and refrigerator. There are 25 different color alternatives.
www.aykasa.com.tr

FOUR BLADE BLENDER SET

Korkmaz shortens the time you spend in the kitchen by providing additional power with the four blade blender set it has developed. Korkmaz, which helps you make more time for yourself with the small home appliances it designs has a new product, the Mia Mega Blender Set that will be your greatest helper in the kitchen. The stainless steel set that comes with blending, whisking, chopping, and grinding functions can be used with convenience on hot and cold dishes. The product comprises four steel chopping blades, a wire whisk, a 1500 ml capacity chopping chamber and 1000 ml capacity measuring cup. The product which has a dual turbo speed setting also contains a stainless steel chopping rod and whisk. The product a non-slip surface also an easily detachable and washable mixing rod. The product comes in pink, lilac, turquoise, and blue colors in vintage hues.
www.korkmaz.com.tr

Bora

Made in Türkiye

100%
BORA
Quality

Premium quality at plastic households
and professional kitchen equipments since 1957...

www.boraplastik.com.tr

Bora Plastik San. ve Tic. A.Ş.
Merkez Cihangir Mah. Petrol Ofisi Caddesi No. 11 34310 Avcılar İstanbul, Türkiye
T +90(212) 422 1850 (pbx)   F +90(212) 422 4434

Şube İstoç Ticaret Merkezi 25. Ada No. 153-155 34550 Mahmutbey İstanbul, Türkiye
T +90(212) 659 5710   F +90(212) 659 5711

LATEST NEWS FROM KITCHENWARE SECTOR

VIKING PROFESSIONAL PRODUCTS

Viking Professional cares about Hygiene as much as its customers care about taste. Prioritizing high hygiene standards are essential for mass consumer markets. Viking Professional's kitchen hygiene portfolio and dosage equipment allows remarkable delicacies to be prepared at the industrial kitchens. Viking Professional Kitchen Hygiene products are developed with R&D experts through state-of-the-art technology and sustainable philosophy. Viking Academy provides theoretical and practical workshops for Viking Professional products and systems. Workshops expose a great advantage to maintain total hygiene and sustainable customer satisfaction. They invite you to try the experience of Viking Professional kitchen hygiene products for the best dishes and service.

www.sailorviking.com

ALL KINDS OF TRAYS

Göreme Melamin which is situated in Istanbul and has a history that goes back to 70s, is one of the pioneers activating in melamine sector. It was founded officially in Bayrampaşa/Istanbul approximately in 1972. The machines operated with manual techniques at the beginning period. Then they were motorized and automated by our own techniques. Actually they currently produce all kinds of trays and new cake covers at the moment.

www.gorememelamin.com.tr

INNOVATION IN THE KITCHEN

Non slip edges, anti-bacterial and anti-odour, sturdy cutting surface, easy clean, knife friendly. Gondol Plastik's new product, a basic non-slip chopping board launches a new era in kitchens, with its newest double injection technology. Diswasher-safe, BPA free, environmentally friendly production, 4 trendy color options (red, purple, pink and yellow) and 2 different sizes (big and small).

www.gondolplastic.com

TRANSPARENT FOOD CONTAINERS

Yeşiller Plastik has collected its kitchenware products under the Açelya brand. Açelya food containers preserve foods in healthy conditions for a long time while offering safe storage for all sorts of items. They are manufactured using polypropylene plastic. Their transparency allows you to see inside it, even when it is inside the fridge. Açelya strainer, dish dryer, and many other kitchen ware objects facilitate your life while adding elegance and aesthetics to your kitchen with their modern design.

www.yesillerplastik.com

nehir

nehir.com.tr

Hot trends

MARKIZ DINING SET FROM EMSAN

The Emsan Markiz Dining Set is hard thanks to the bone dust in its content, and scratch resistant with its transparent nature. It brings elegance to your tables with its pattern embossed on white porcelain, and its golden embellishments. You can serve your loved ones in crowded dining tables with the simple and elegant design of the Markiz Dining Set for 12.

www.emsan.com.tr

A GOLDEN TOUCH IN THE KITCHEN

GOLD HAS BEEN ACCEPTED AS THE MOST APPARENT INDICATION OF WEALTH THROUGHOUT HISTORY. THIS GOLD MEETS WHITE, AND SOMETIMES STEEL, CREATING A LOVELY LOOK IN YOUR KITCHEN, CREATING QUALITY. WE HAVE TAKEN A LOOK AT PRODUCTS THAT BRING A GLIMMER TO THE KITCHEN FOR YOU.

GLIMMERING TABLES FROM KORKMAZ

Korkmaz, which has manufactured stainless steel kitchenware and household appliances since 1972 has managed to continuously develop its manufacturing capacity with state of the art technology, succeeding in extending its current market position to a larger area. Human health is foremost among the criteria which guide Korkmaz's vision. All products are compliant with international norms of health and quality. Korkmaz which also moves ahead with significant steps in foreign trade relations exports to nearly 80 countries. Korkmaz's Lyda Swing cutlery set comprises 89 pieces and is offered for sale in its special leather box.

www.korkmaz.com.tr

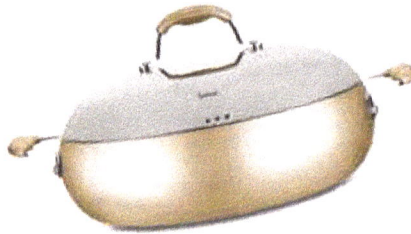

CERAMIC COATED POT FROM HİSAR

Hisar which has embraced the principle of high quality manufacturing of cutlery and steel cookware, manufactures its products from 304 stainless steel alloyed with 18/10 chromium-nickel. Products come with a factory guarantee against corrosion, and are offered for use after undergoing a careful quality control process. Hisar equips its factories with computer controlled modern machinery and equipment which minimizes manufacturing errors, and Hisar's Mercury ceramic coated cookware set displays the finest example of the combination of white and gold with its gold handles and white lid.

www.hisar.com.tr

A RETURN TO THE 70'S FROM PORLAND

The Bohemian collection of Porland –which itself was first established in 1976- inspired by the spirit of the 70's and the romance of the 50's has its prominent themes in bohemian elegance, the unique harmony of gold with white, a positive romantic effect, and the colors and patterns freely displayed by the theatrical atmosphere born of the use of two different patterns. The Bohem (Bohemian) collection of Porland comprising a dining set, tea and coffee service sets manufactured of the patented and trademarked Alumilite porcelain which combines the creamy color of soft porcelain and the durability of hard porcelain, includes an interpretation of two different patterns which have been aged using only golden gilt, creating an amorphous effect.

www.porland.com.tr

For colorful kitchens **NOUVAL**

NOUVAL GROUP MUTFAK EŞYALARI DIŞ TİC. LTD. ŞTİ.

facebook.com/nouval.tr
twitter.com/NOUVALGROUP

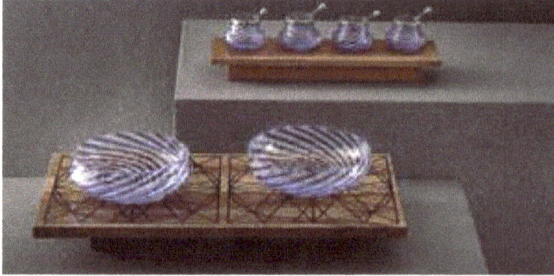

CHESM-İ SÜMBÜL

Pasabahçe which continues to combine design with glass has offered its new collection "Omnia" in which it designs the future of glass by interpreting the wealth of Anatolian culture with modern lines to the appreciation of glass enthusiasts. Paşabahçe's Chesm-i Sümbül Spice Set bears the signature of designer Ali Bakova, who used lids in traditional Çeşm-i Bülbül using them outside their original purpose, by turning them upside down and converting them into a tabletop service set for salt-pepper-oregano-dried mint.
www.pasabahce.com.tr

SPICES AND SPICE CRUETS

SPICES THAT IMBUE DISHES AND THE FOOD CULTURE TO WHICH THEY BELONG WITH AN IDENTITY ARE ESPECIALLY INDISPENSABLE FOR US IN TURKEY. THUS, SPICE CRUETS MUST ALWAYS BE AT OUR FINGERTIPS, AT THE MOST EASILY ACCESSIBLE POINT OF OUR KITCHEN.

BILARDO SPICE SERVICE

The Jumbo Bilardo spice service manufactured of stainless steel has three semi-spherical compartments. While round metal lids perfectly complement the design of the tri-compartment main structure, creating a global design and look. Cylindrical holders mounted on the lids create a holistic look with the rod and holder mounted on the main body. The Bilardo spice service has lesser risk of overturning since it contacts the table at three points, and in addition to enabling spices to be easily carried with a single move, create a more clutter-free and elegant look in the kitchen or on the table. The lids with their convenient use allow comfort while rendering the design more elegant with their visual appeal.
www.jumbo.com.tr

GLASS SPICE JARS WITH COLORFUL LIDS

Es Kalıp San. ve Tic. Ltd. Şti. which was founded in 2004, and serves the house and table wares sector under the Eminem brand manufactures glass kitchen and table wares. In addition to being healthy for their glass material, Eminem spice jars are visually appealing for their different and colorful lids.
www.eminem.com.tr

YOUR KITCHEN'S CHEF

Obje Plastik which is one of the fastest developing manufacturing and exporting companies of Turkey in the plastics sector since its founding in 2007 has a product range of over 200 products in the plastics kitchen and house wares sector. Obje Plastik, which operates with 50 employees on 4 thousand square meters offers the Şef salt and spice service, which is remarkable for its high quality elegance and convenience. The Şef salt and spice service is waiting to be the chef of your kitchen, on lovingly prepared tables.
www.objeplastik.com

MADE IN TURKEY

Quality | Design | Competitive Price | Flexibility

evsid

Turkish Houseware Manufacturers Association

Pls contact with us for the full list of **Turkish Housewares manufacturers.**

Pls contact with us for the full list of **Turkish Housewares manufacturers.**

Ev ve Mutfak Eşyaları Sanayicileri ve İhracatçıları Derneği

Turkish Housewares Manufacturers Association

İstoç 50. Yol No: 2 / 84 Toptancılar Çarşısı C plaza 8.Kat No:67 Mahmutbey Bağcılar/İstanbul/TÜRKİYE

T: +90 212 659 94 25 F: +90 212 659 94 20 www.evsid.org.tr - evsid@evsid.org.tr

Türkiye Discover the potential

www.porland.com.tr

"PORLAND IS A WORLD BRAND"

ESEN KARATEKİN, PORLAND CORPORATE COMMUNICATION EXECUTIV STATES THAT THEY CATER TO THE WORLD MARKET AS PORLAND, ANE ADDS, "WE THEREFORE CONDUCT SIGNIFICANT RESEARCH ON KITCHE REQUIREMENTS BORN OF CULTURAL DIFFERENCES."

E sen Karatekin stated that they carry out 100% local production, and most importantly manufacture under healthy, and hygienic conditions, and told us about Porland.

WOULD YOU TELL OF YOUR COMPANY'S FOUNDING PROCESS?

Today Porland, which employs over 1500 people with its porcelain production as well as its other brands in its portfolio, is a significant player which exports 65 percent of its production volume to over 30 counties on four continents in the world with a manufacturing capacity of nearly 70 million items a year, more than 20 stores within Turkey, regional directorates catering to the horeca market, and many sales points; and the great portion of this success belongs no doubt to Süleyman Pamukçu who has transformed his commercial life into a success story by working hard with the dream and ambition of becoming a world brand. The closing down of İstanbul Porselen in 1990 which was Porland's major supplier laid the foundation of its current manufacturing identity. It established

Porland Porselen Sanayi ve Tic. A.Ş. in 1992 and carried out its first porcelain production at its factory in Gebze. Subsequently, the Bilecik manufacturing plant was commissioned in 1996 with an outdoor space of 300 thousand square meters and an indoor space of 70 thousand square meters. Today marketing operations of products manufactured with Porland Porselen are still carried out by İmge İhracat ve İthalat Şirketi that is housed under the same roof.

HOW DO YOU CREATE NEW DESIGNS? DO YOU HAVE A R&D DEPARTMENT?

All products we offer to the market can be bought as sets or as individual pieces. In the same way, we will be working to achieve long term sustainability of our quality criteria which we have developed, including mechanical strength, surface hardness, and the advantage of 100% local production.

WOULD YOU TELL US OF THE INVESTMENTS YOU MADE IN 2015?

We have enjoyed the pride of opening the largest store of our sector on an area of 3000 square meters in

Vialand SC. Similarly, the number and quality of our foreign connectio and our sales points have increased significantly, on the road to becomin a world brand. We have reinforced our American, Asian, and European market with the Middle East in spec projects. Aside from these, we have introduced innovative products that keep the pulse of the market with th consumer one after the other, with o manufacturing identity. Our Alumil (Porcelain with Alumina) porcelain products which we have developed a a result of three years of R&D work have achieved the desired effect botl horeaca and in retail.

WOULD YOU TELL US OF YOUR PRODU VARIETIES?

We have a target product group i porcelain which we can divide into two sub-groups. These are horeca (professional) and household produ We design our gastronomy products considering the expectations and ne of the sector. We manufacture differe designs and forms for different worl cuisines. Our gastronomy consumer can purchase the products without patterns or decorations, and can also purchase them with special logos, an patterns upon demand. Our househc products include tabletop products s as products used in the preparation stage, cookware, service products, decorative and gift products, bathro products, and accessories.

DO YOU HAVE OVERSEAS DEALERSHII

We conduct most of our foreign sales via our dealers. However, hotels and restaurants sometimes purchase directly from us.

Grandeur®
Non Stick Process

V Model
Soft Granite Series

living
innovation

Savaşan Emaye ve Soba Sanayi Ltd. Şti.
Tatlıcak Mah. Taştepe Sk. No: 36/1
Karatay - Konya - Türkiye
Tel: +90.332 334 05 50 (pbx)
Fax: +90.332 334 05 60
www.savasan.com
savasan@savasan.com

By SAVASAN

"EXPORT TO MORE THAN 65 COUNTRIES"

SONER ARSLAN SAYS, EGE EXPORTS TO MORE THAN 65 COUNTRIES AND ITS PRIMARY OBJECTIVE IS TO BECOME ONE OF THE TOP 1000 EXPORTERS OF TURKEY.

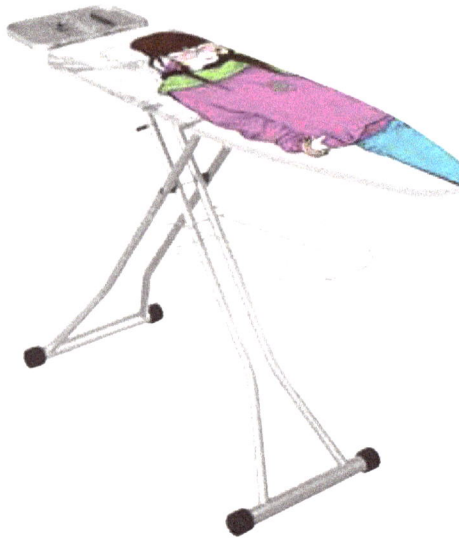

www.egeevurunleri.com.tr

Ege Ev A.Ş Export Manager Soner Arslan answered Turkish Kitchenware's questions.

HOW LONG HAVE YOU BEEN IN THIS SECTOR? WOULD YOU TELL US BRIEFLY OF YOUR COMPANY'S FOUNDING PROCESS?

Ege Ev Ürünleri A.Ş (EGE HOME PRODUCTS) has been established in İzmir/Turkey and effectively serving to costumer's need since 1996. From beginning to now, company has expanded capacity and improved quality while following customer satisfaction policy.

HOW DO YOU CREATE NEW DESIGNS? DO YOU HAVE A R&D DEPARTMENT?

We have a strong Ar-Ge department whichworks in harmony with fabric designers, brochure designers and Plastic and Metal mould departments in our own structure. Strong colloboration of these units drive us to the top during the creative process.

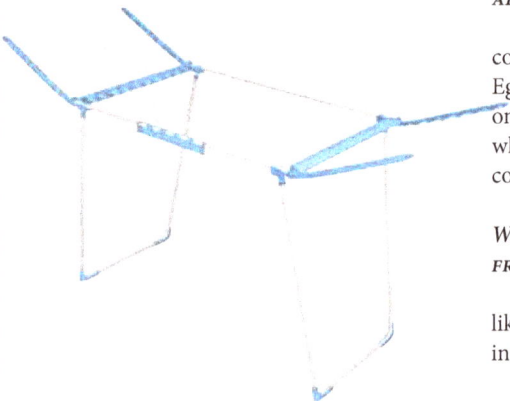

WOULD YOU TELL US OF THE INVESTMENTS YOU MADE IN 2015?

We believe that the biggest investment is good workers for a strong company. Ege improve the quality with qualified workers and continuous improvements on factory production capability

DO YOU EXPORT, AND WHAT ARE THE COUNTRIES IN YOUR PORTFOLIO? WOULD YOU GIVE US INFORMATION ABOUT YOUR EXPORT FIGURES?

Ege currently exports to over 65 countries all around the world currently. Ege's primary objective is to become one of the top 1000 exporters of Turkey, which is a very achievable objective considering our current export figures.

WHAT KIND OF FEEDBACK DO YOU GET FROM FAIRS YOU ATTEND?

We attend many International fairs like Ambiente, Chicago, Hong Kong and in Turkey like Zuchex and Ideal Home, which creates many opportunuties to meet with our potential and current costumers. We were happy to be in these fairs for years and we will continue to be there in 2016.

WOULD YOU TELL US OF YOUR PRODUCT VARIETIES?

Ironing boards, clothes dryers and ladders are main products that we have focused to be unbeatable manufactuer of Turkey. We have wide variety of these products in our production line as we serve all the levels of the market.

DO YOU HAVE OVERSEAS DEALERSHIPS?

We have strong distribution channels and sole agents in some countries as Germany, Algeria, Austria, Kazakhstan, Saudi Arabia, etc... Beside we have our own Office and sale persons in Russia.

WHAT DO YOUR PLANS FOR THE FUTURE ENTAIL?

We are mainly aiming to make stronger our influence in export markets by creating new success stories in new regions. As we said "we are, where you are".

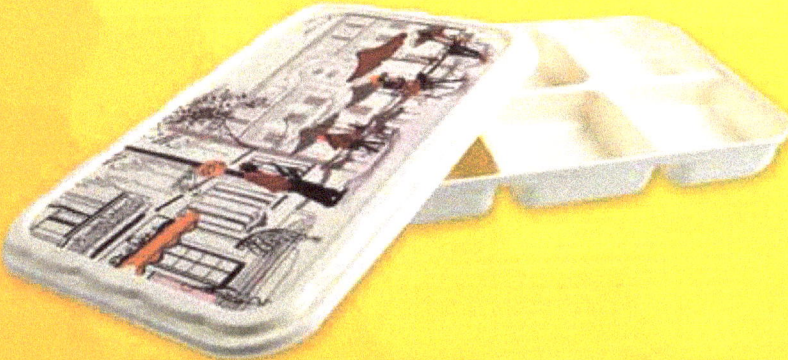

GRM®

Quality is not coincidence...

www.gorememelamin.com.tr

GÖREME
Melamin

İstoç 10. Ada No:59 Bağcılar / İstanbul
Tel: 0212 659 84 41 Fax: 0212 659 84 39 - Mail: info@gorememelamin.com.tr

"RENGA IS A CUSTOMER ORIENTED MANAGEMENT"

CENK ALBAYRAK SAYS THAT, THEIR PLAN IS TO ENTER SOME OF COUNTRIES ESPECIALLY IN THE CENTRAL AFRICAN AND SCANDINAVIAN REGION OF EUROPE.

www.renga.com.tr

Mercanlar Kitchen-Renga Deputy General Manager Cenk Albayrak answered Turkish Kitchenware's questions.

HOW LONG HAVE YOU BEEN IN THIS SECTOR? WOULD YOU TELL US BRIEFLY OF YOUR COMPANY'S FOUNDING PROCESS?

Our company is in this area of busines for more than 15 years, due to the right investments and customer oriented management we have become one of the most reliable supplier of glassware kitchen items in the world.

HOW DO YOU CREATE NEW DESIGNS? DO YOU HAVE A R&D DEPARTMENT?

We have our own r&d department which is developing our new designs and innovating the current ones as per the demand of various markets that we have.

WOULD YOU TELL US OF THE INVESTMENTS YOU MADE IN 2015?

Along with some new items we recently produced which have been aprroved by the accredited organizations such as SGS and INETERTEK, due to the well-organized quality and production facilities we are also confirmed to have ISO 90001certificate.

DO YOU EXPORT, AND WHAT ARE THE COUNTRIES IN YOUR PORTFOLIO? WOULD YOU GIVE US INFORMATION ABOUT YOUR EXPORT FIGURES?

We are exporting to many of countries from South America to far east and from northest region of Russia to South Africa.

WHAT KIND OF FEEDBACK DO YOU GET FROM FAIRS YOU ATTEND?

We either make contracts with some of our customers already during the fair or keep negotiation after the fair to consider their additional demands and do our best for matching with the expectation of market.

WOULD YOU TELL US OF YOUR PRODUCT VARIETIES?

Glass Kitchenware items with plastic accessories, plastic tableware items and bambu&metal Kitchenware items.

DO YOU HAVE OVERSEAS DEALERSHIPS?

Yes we have some exclusive customers in some certain countries.

WHAT DO YOUR PLANS FOR THE FUTURE ENTAIL?

Our plan is to enter some of countries especially in Middle Africa and Scandinavian Region of Europe. Our main goal is to develop easy use & innovated kitchenware items with reosanable amount, we consider the demand & life style of many different markets which allows us to keep and supply such a big product range.

Mia Manolya

KORKMAZ

Taste & Beyond

GRANITE

Excellent scratch-proof interior granite and high-temperature resistant exterior materials allow you to cook special meals with ease. Perspiration-enhancing ecological, environment-friendly materials are used for the production of Mia Manolya.

Google play
Korkmaz Catalog App available on Google Play

App Store
Korkmaz Catalog App available on App Store

www.korkmaz.com.tr

"WE HAVE ALWAYS EXISTED WITH OUR QUALITY"

CENK KAVUKÇU, EXECUTIVE DIRECTOR OF KAVSAN STRESSES THAT KAVSAN HAD COMPLETED 30 YEARS IN THE SECTOR, AND HAD CARRIED OUT HIGH QUALITY PRODUCTION THROUGHOUT THIS PERIOD, AND SAYS, "WE HAVE EMBRACED THE MISSION OF ALWAYS BEING THE FIRST ONES TO MANUFACTURE A PRODUCT."

www.kavsan.com.tr

Cenk Kavukçu says, "Kavsan's name in the sector is equivalent to trust," and adds, "Now we are moving forward with our new child, Zucci." We have conducted an interview with Cenk Kavukçu.

How long have you been in this sector? Would you tell us briefly of your company's founding process?

Our experience in the sector which began as a company with multiple partners in 1975 has continued under our title of Kavsan Plastik ve Metal San. Tic. Ltd. Şti. since 1987. The founder of our company, Cihan Kavukçu is a doyenne of the sector and Kavsan's greatest advantage in achieving its current state. Cihan Kavukçu is known in our sector as a person who is in love with production, and his name inspires trust in the sector. Thanks to this advantage, Kavsan has taught its employees and the sector its production stance that does not waver in quality, and the essential nature of being honest and reliable, and has built its corporate personality on these facts. Therefore Kavsan's name in the sector is equivalent to trust."

Would you give us information about your production figures and business volume?

Our aim is to always manufacture the newest and most different. We have embraced the emission of always being the first ones to manufacture something. An average of 10-12 thousand products come out of our manufacturing facility per day, and after packaging and quality control, are offered for sale. We have a total capacity to process around 200-220 tons of raw materials on an average monthly bases in all our product lines.

How do you create new designs? Do you have a R&D department?

Our R&D department is headed by our company owner Cihan Kavukçu who is a designer himself, and 35-40 percent of Kavsan products are born of his drawings.

Would you tell us of the investments you made in 2015?

2015 is the year in which Zucci, Kevsan's largest investment to date was born. We are combining Kavsan's vast experience and great power gathered through the years with Zucci's innovative and aesthetic bearing. Kavsan is completing 30 years in the sector, and has been carrying out high quality production throughout this period. Despite these 30 years, we are always open to new perspectives, new visions. We are now moving ahead with our new child, Zucci.

Do you export, and what are the countries in your portfolio? Would you give us information about your export figures?

Export has always been a priority for Kavsan. Our company made its first export in 1994. 2014 and 2015 were very important year in terms of our exports. Turkey's place in the last decade as well as our mutual relationships with different countries that are growing on a daily basis, the clearing of the way for the African market, and the economic situations of European countries have added to our speed. Our aim for 2016 for both Kavsan and our new brand Zucci is to double our export potential.

Would you tell us of your product varieties?

Our portfolio comprises 200 product varieties. We currently serve our customers as Kavsan, with the manufacture of plastic, metal, wood, and ceramic products. Gathering such a large number of different materials and raw materials, different manufacturing methods, and such a diverse production track has been a long process for us. But at the completion of this process we are capable of contract manufacturing for our customers be it for the purposes of sale, or under their own brands. If we would summarize the basic attributes of Kavsan branded products, this word would be "quality."

Mia Duo

KORKMAZ

Taste & Beyond

850 W

850 W

Mia Duo Blender, its features speed at its strength and heat resistant. Stainless steel blades which will be your best friend helper in the kitchen while cooking for grinding, shredding the food.

Google play
Korkmaz Catalog App
available on Google Play

App Store
Korkmaz Catalog App
available on App Store

www.korkmaz.com.tr

"EMINEM IS CREATING A NEW PRODUCT RANGE"

EMINEM EXPORT MANAGER RAHMİ KAŞIKÇI STATES THAT THEY ASSIGN HIGHEST PRIORITY FOR THEIR NEW PRODUCT DESIGNS TO PRODUCTS THAT WILL MAKE LIFE EASIER AND ADD VALUE TO KITCHENS.

www.eminem.com.tr

Rahmi Kaşıkçı stated that it was possible to find Eminem products in markets and bazaars in many Mid-Eastern countries, and answered our questions.

WOULD YOU TELL US BRIEFLY OF YOUR COMPANY'S FOUNDING PROCESS?

Our company began production of glass and plastic kitchen wares in 2004, on an area of 5 thousand square meters in Istanbul. Our showroom at İstoç Block 12 Nr. 62 opened at the same time, and this is where we run our marketing network.

HOW DO YOU CREATE NEW DESIGNS? DO YOU HAVE A R&D DEPARTMENT?

We implement projects for new products by considering changing living conditions, and in accordance with the wishes and demands of customers, And we have ongoing projects. We create our new product projects in the form of a product family. We will serially produce salt shakers, spice and oil cruets and jar containers. We have a R&D department. We assign first priority in designing new products to products that will make life easier and that will add value to our kitchens.

WOULD YOU TELL US OF THE INVESTMENTS YOU MADE IN 2015?

In 2015, through our expansion efforts on our factory, we combined our two factories under a single roof. We have taken our production under control. We have also renovated our İSTOÇ showroom, and split it into two sections as export and local market sales.

DO YOU EXPORT, AND WHAT ARE THE COUNTRIES IN YOUR PORTFOLIO? WOULD YOU GIVE US INFORMATION ABOUT YOUR EXPORT FIGURES?

We aim to export to various countries with the local and foreign fairs we have attended, and we plan to attend. Today, it is possible to see our products in markets and bazaars of many Mid-Eastern countries. We are of the opinion that we are successful in exporting to all Mid-Eastern countries. We are aiming for the Sub-Saharan countries, as well as the markets we have not yet been able to access in South America and Europe.

WOULD YOU TELL US OF YOUR PRODUCT VARIETIES?

Our products comprise two sections which are glass and plastic products. Our glass products group includes cruets, salt and spice shakers, pitchers, and glass containers. We can group our plastic products as functional plastic containers, pitchers, soap dispensers, and spoon holders.

DO YOU HAVE OVERSEAS DEALERSHIPS?

We have dealers in several countries where we operate. We will assign greater importance to our dealership efforts in 2016.

WHAT DO YOUR PLANS FOR 2016 ENTAIL?

We shall open 2016 with the Ambiente – Germany fair. The fair will be followed by planned visits to several countries. Our company will become more popular through the new products we have designed.

Korkmaz Vertex Deep Fryer, which has removable oil container, lid and filter preventing the oil spread. Vertex provides the sensation of variety and easy frying.

Google play
Korkmaz Catalog App available on Google Play

App Store
Korkmaz Catalog App available on App Store

www.korkmaz.com.tr

"2015 HAS BEEN A YEAR OF INVESTMENT FOR US"

ÜNAL DEMIR, CHAIRMAN OF THE BOARD OF EXECUTIVES OF SANAT TOPRAK ÜRÜNLERI STATES THAT THEY HAD INVESTED IN MOLDS FOR NEW COLLECTIONS AND ADDED NEW EQUIPMENT TO THEIR MACHINE PARK IN 2015.

www.sanattoprak.com.tr

We have conversed about Sanat Toprak Ürünleri AŞ with Ünal Demir who states that they export 77 percent of their production.

WOULD YOU TELL US BRIEFLY OF YOUR COMPANY'S FOUNDING PROCESS?

In its production adventure which began in 2003 in the table wares sector, Sanat Toprak Ürünleri AŞ Porselen is currently one of our country's leading exporters. It continues its production on an indoor area of 17 thousand square meters, set on 90 thousand square meters in the Pazaryeri Organized Industrial Zone in Bilecik. The SNT brand was derived from our main company, Sanat. The manufacturing process which employs a total of 500 people does not compromise on international standards in work safety, worker's health, and environmental impacts.

HOW DO YOU CREATE NEW DESIGNS? DO YOU HAVE A R&D DEPARTMENT?

Various product development efforts in accordance with customer demands in terms of forms and different colors are carried out by the product development department. We are also conducting a new product development project jointly ran by Product Development and R&D. Work is being carried out on a new product from the stoneware family, which we describe as a transparent material. We will offer this product group which is striking in terms of aesthetics and elegance, and dazzling for its off-white color and its gleam for the enjoyment of consumers as well. We have also observed that our products created with reactive glazes we had previously developed have enjoyed a significant

response from the market. We aim to meet new product lines and colors with new relief works in this area, and continue to offer them for the enjoyment of our customers.

DO YOU EXPORT, AND WHAT ARE THE COUNTRIES IN YOUR PORTFOLIO? WOULD YOU GIVE US INFORMATION ABOUT YOUR EXPORT FIGURES?

We export to a range of countries from Europe to America. Also, Egypt which is called the door to Africa is one of our new albeit not very regular export markets. We currently export 77% of our products.

When we look at their share in our exports, stoneware products are predominantly exported while porcelain is predominantly sold to the local market.

WHAT KIND OF FEEDBACK DO YOU GET FROM FAIRS YOU ATTEND?

The local Zuchex fair, and the overseas Ambiente fairs which are significant for

our sector, are among the fairs which we attend. We promote our brand by participating in fairs, and telling people about SNT. We are expanding our customer portfolio.

WOULD YOU TELL US OF YOUR PRODUCT VARIETIES?

Our products comprise two main branches within the tableware sector. One is household products, while the other is the service sector known as HORECA. As SNT, we manufacture both stoneware and porcelain to meet the requirements of both segments. Our basic criteria in developing products that will meet the requirements of both sectors are aesthetic appeal and functionality.

WHAT DO YOUR PLANS FOR 2016 ENTAIL?

We have made new investments as dictated by the needs that emerged due to customer demands in stoneware. In porcelain we had completed our investment plan considering market demand, and decided to invest in this direction. In 2015 we have begun investment in construction, and we are near completion. Our porcelain investment is being made by Azur Porselen AŞ which is a member of our group of companies. We aim to reach a capacity of 18,000,000 units/ year with our technologically renewed manufacturing process at our new factory with an indoor area of 10,000 square meters. We will complete this process within 2016.

Zucci

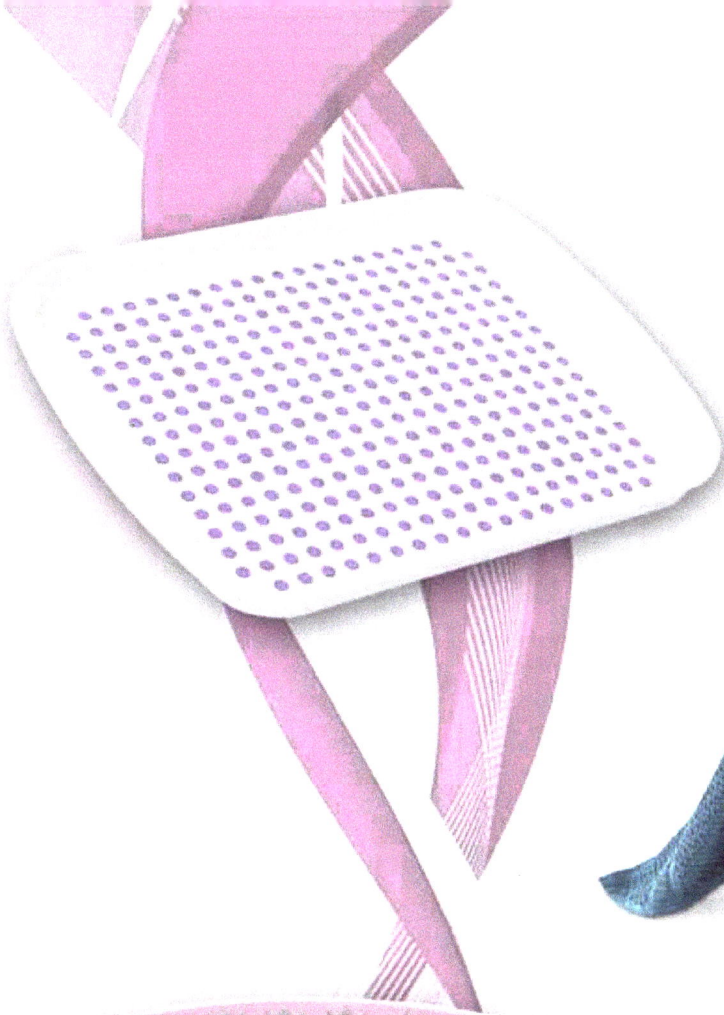

UKS
ISO 22000:2005

Global
ISO 9001

UKAS
039

Turkey
Discover
the potential

KAVSAN
Plastik ve Metal San. Tic. Ltd. Şti.

Factory: Merkez Mah.
Prof. Dr. M. Nevzat Pisak Cad.
No:4/1 İç Kapı No:10
Yenibosna / İstanbul - TÜRKİYE
Tel: +90 (212) 552 01 38 - 451 42 28
Fax: +90 (212) 552 40 71
www.kavsan.com

Branch: İstoç Z Blok No:95
Bağcılar / İSTANBUL
Tel: +90 212 659 45 82
Fax: +90 212 659 37 81
kavsan@kavsan.com

www.zucci.com.tr

"WE SELL 60% OF OUR PRODUCTS IN THE INTERNATIONAL AREA"

AS THE FIRST COMPANY TO MOLD THEIR OWN MELAMINE IN KITCHEN PRODUCTS MARKET, GÖREME MELAMINE WHICH WAS SET UP IN 1970, IS PROGRESSING BY EXPANDING ITS EXPORT TARGETS.

W e interviewed Hüseyin Cengiz who is a partner of Göreme Melamine Plastics & Bakalite Industry, about the company, the products of this company and their goals in foreign markets.

CAN YOU INTRODUCE YOUR COMPANY TO US BRIEFLY? WOULD YOU LIKE TO GIVE US SOME INFORMATION ABOUT THE ACTIVITIES OF THE COMPANY?

Göreme Melamin which is situated in Istanbul and has a history that goes back to 70s, is one of the pioneers activating in melamine sector. It was founded officially in Bayrampaşa/Istanbul approximately in 1972. The machines operated with arm techniques at the beginning period. Then they were motorized and chained by our own techniques. At that time, there were five pressing machines on operation. There were not many producers in melamine sector at that time and the moulds used to be imported from Italy as they were not being made in Turkey. Göreme Melamine was the first company which produced its own moulds. This work was realized by 12 people and now

www.gorememelamin.com.tr

we produce all kinds of kitchen goods and services.

HOW ABOUT THE PERFORMANCE OF YOUR COMPANY IN 2015? CAN YOU TELL THE GOALS OF YOUR FIRM ABOUT THIS YEAR AND NEXT YEAR?

We will be have more items in a short time. Because we have been obtaining new technologies both for domestic and international projects. In 2015, we took place in at the fairs in İstanbul. These had a good effect on our work. Because of it , we came in contact with our new clients. When our negotiations are over, we will

produce a variety of items both for kitchen and bathroom.

WILL YOU SUPPLY NEW PRODUCTS TO FOREIGN MARKETS THIS YEAR?

Actually we produce all kinds of trays and new cake covers at the moment. We are quite popular regarding this field. These are sold due to new designs and its quality. That is why they prefer us.

HOW ABOUT YOUR PRODUCTION CAPACITY? AND DO YOU HAVE NEW INVESTMENT PLANS?

Monthly, we produce 70-80 tons melamine for Turkey and for abroad. We will move to a larger space in a short time. And then we will develop us more efficiently for next year.

WHAT IS YOUR PRODUCT RANGE?

At the moment we have got 10 items. But we will have more in a short time, because technologie is developing and this brings more possibilities for us. Our outstanding products are trays and new cake covers.

WHAT IS THE SHARE OF YOUR PRODUCTION IN DOMESTIC AND OVERSEAS MARKETS?

In the past, 70 % of our products were sold in Turkey and 30 % of it were sold abroad. Now it has changed because we have new items. At the moment, I can say that we sell 60 % of our products in international area and 40 % of it in Turkey's market.

WHICH COUNTRIES ARE YOU MAINLY EXPORTING TO? WHICH ARE YOUR TARGET COUNTRIES?

We export our goods to the Middle East and to European area. And now we would like to have more clients in South America and another continents.

ÖZTİRYAKİLER IS IN THE TOP FIVE IN EUROPE

IN ADDITION TO BEING LEADER OF THE DOMESTIC MARKET IN THE INDUSTRIAL KITCHEN SECTOR, ÖZTIRYAKILER WHICH HAS A WIDE MARKETING AND AFTERSALES SERVICE NETWORK WITH FOUR REGIONAL DIRECTORATES, 50 DEALERS, AND 80 AUTHORIZED SERVICE STATIONS IN TURKEY RANKS IN THE TOP FIVE COMPANIES IN EUROPE AND IN THE TOP 15 IN THE WORLD.

www.oztiryakiler.com.tr

We have had an interview with Tahsin Öztiryaki, Vice Chairman of the Executive Board of Öztiryakiler who states that they had also opened what is the first R&D Center in the sector in last November.

HOW LONG HAVE YOU BEEN IN THIS SECTOR? WOULD YOU TELL US BRIEFLY OF YOUR COMPANY'S FOUNDING PROCESS?

Öztiryakiler has set the technologic course of the sector since 1958, as one of Turkey's first manufacturing firms in the industrial kitchen sector. With its 1300 employees in 10 group companies, on 130 thousand square meters of indoor manufacturing area at its manufacturing facilities in Turkey and Russia, it is one of the largest players in the market.

WOULD YOU TELL US ABOUT YOUR PRODUCTION AND YOUR PRODUCTION FACILITIES?

Öztiryakiler serves in 108 countries on five continents via distribution channels and authorized service stations. It has showrooms and warehouses housing sales-marketing and project teams in Kazakhstan and Russia, and a manufacturing facility in Russia with 10 thousand square meters of indoor space. The firm which manufactured over 4,500 varieties of product for the gastronomy sector has over 10 thousand product varieties including the products it imports and the products it sells to the domestic market. Öztiryakiler products are sold with the OZTI brand and the "Made in Turkey" stamp in 108 countries. Öztiryakiler is also the kitchenware supplier of the armed forces of many countries with its productions in portable field products.

HOW DO YOU CREATE NEW DESIGNS? DO YOU HAVE A R&D DEPARTMENT?

Öztiryakiler which sets the technologic course of the industrial kitchen sector has established the first R&D Center with the sense of responsibility of being the leader of the sector. The center which is also the only R&D Center of the sector, equipped with all the skills and infrastructure needed to design industrial kitchen equipment from start to finish, develop and test the equipment opened last November.

WOULD YOU TELL US OF THE INVESTMENTS YOU MADE IN 2015? WHAT ARE YOU PLANNING FOR 2016?

While we included new dealers in the domestic market, we also began working with new countries. This year, we have created a reaction in the market as a brand by increasing our product figures and by offering quality at more affordable prices. Our domestic sales have increased in parallel to this. We have achieved not only a price advantage, but also a cost advantage by making our products of higher quality, more streamlined, and faster. We are more hopeful of 2016 in terms of export and the domestic market. When we look in terms of our sector, Turkey will have a better year in 2016.

Chef

"TURKEY IS A LUCKY COUNTRY IN TERMS OF FOOD"

Chef Mehmet Siriş who has set his heart on the profession of cooking for 30 years says theirs is a difficult job and adds, "If you absorb this difficulty, accept and enjoy it, cooking a bad dish counts as a defeat for you."

WHEN AND HOW DID YOU FIRST BECOME INTERESTED IN COOKING?

I entered the kitchen to help out when I was in high school, and I have not been able to leave it since.

HOW DID YOU DEVELOP YOURSELF IN THIS AREA?

I think it is ideological. While I was not overly fond of the service part, which I had started with enthusiasm, I thought I should be a master of a marketable skill. I had to be an artisan, and do higher quality work than everyone else. In other words, I had to create awareness. I entered the kitchen with that ambition. For 30 years we have roamed the world. This is an adventure that still goes on, even though we don't know where it will end.

HAVE YOU RECEIVED AN EDUCATION ON COOKING?

Education is indispensable for mankind in every sense. I have had a lot of professional, and academic education. The first step in creating the food is the order, and the cold chain that is part of the order. Storage before the product has gone bad, processing, and timely presentation. We call these "HACCP Steps" (Hazard Analysis and Critical Control Point)." I have received many training courses in cooking, chopping, color matching, calorie scales as well as in techniques for safety in the kitchen that are offshoot of these, and I am still learning to meet the standards of the globalizing world.

MEHMET SİRİŞ

CHEF MEHMET SİRİŞ THINKS TURKEY IS A LUCKY COUNTRY FOR ITS HISTORICAL AND CULTURAL PAST AS WELL AS ANATOLIA'S AMENABLE LOCATION FOR AGRICULTURE AND ANIMAL HUSBANDRY, AND THE FACT THAT ALL TYPES OF VEGETABLES AND FRUITS GROW HERE.

WHEN WAS YOUR FIRST PROFESSIONAL FOOD-RELATED JOB? WHERE DID YOU WORK?

I can say that, my experience which lasted nearly 10 years at the Çırağan Palace Hotel Kempinski Istanbul was my first academy which directed the course of my life, and added a lot to my life. Afterwards I worked at Mövenpick Istanbul Hotel. During the course of my career, I had the chance to be a chief cook at the Barcelo Eresin

Topkapı Hotel. Then came experience overseas and in chain hotels around the world. Having completed that as well, I returned home. I wished to transfer my knowledge and experience to a new generation in my country, as required by my consciousness of my social responsibility, I proceeded on this road with the Holiday Inn Airport brand of the Intercontinental Hotel Group. After completing the opening of Hilton Kozyatağı and practiced my profession for nearly 1 year at the Martı Hotel Taksim, I retired.

WHAT DO YOU THINK ARE THE BASIC ATTRIBUTES OF TURKISH CUISINE?

In fact our country is a lucky one for its historical and cultural past as well as Anatolia's amenable location for agriculture and animal husbandry, and the fact that all types of vegetables and fruits grow here. I think Turkish cuisine gets its basic features from these conditions as well as the 6 century heritage of the Ottoman Empire.

WHAT IN YOUR OPINION IS THE SECRET TO COOKING WELL?

We have a very difficult job. If you absorb and enjoy this difficulty, cooking poorly is a defeat for you.

Tapasturka

Ingredients:
- ½ scored calamari
- 2 cheese balls dipped in poppy seeds
- 2 salmon wrapped in crêpes
- 1 large shrimp
- 2 meatballs
- 2 tablespoons of tomato sauce
- 5 slices of smoked meat
- 1 breadstick
- 2 tablespoons of soy sauce
- 2 tablespoons of sweet & chili sauce

Lightly score the calamari and cook in the pan in a round shape and serve with soy sauce. Mix feta cheese with cream cheese, shape into balls, cover with poppy seeds and place on skewers. Lay smoked salmon on crepes, roll, and cut. Lay sweet & chili sauce at the bottom, fry the meatballs in a pan, than in the oven, and place on skewers. Serve with tomato sauce. Finally roll smoked meat with the breadstick like cutting pastrami, and serve as in the picture.

Veal tuffahiye

Ingredients:
- 150 g veal sirloin
- 1 green apple
- 2 tablespoons of oil
- 15 g of brown sugar
- 1 green pepper
- 2 tablespoons of almond pilaf
- 2 cherry tomatoes

Preparation:
Cook the meat in a hot pan with salt and pepper, cook apple slices in the same pan and place them on the meat. Serve with almond pilaf, grilled tomatoes, and pepper.

Caramel profiteroles

Ingredients:
- 4 profiterole balls
- 2 tablespoons of caramel sauce
- 1 physalis
- 1 raspberry
- 2 cranberry
- Chocolate sauce for decoration
- 1 piece of crunchy cookie
- Sour cherry sauce

Preparation:
Lightly caramelize sugar, add cream, which gets you the caramel sauce. Fill into the profiterole balls as desired. Serve as in the picture.

Design & designer

SEVİN COŞKUN

"OUR VISION IS TO CREATE PRODUCTS"

SEVİN COŞKUN SAYS THAT, TURKEY'S VISION IS TO CREATE PRODUCTS THAT COMBINE ARTISTIC CONCEPTS.

Designer Sevin Coşkun answered Turkish Kitchenware's questions.

WHO IS SEVİN COŞKUN AND HOW DID SHE STEP INTO THE DESIGN WORLD?

In 2004, after I graduated from METU, I started to work freelance on industrial design projects with my current business partner Mustafa Emre Olur. In 2005 IMMIB organized its first design competition, where we received the second prize with a cutlery set and third prize with a cookware set, in the professional category. At that time, the culture and awareness of design, as well as the understanding of the definition of this profession was insufficient in the industries and winning prizes at a product design competition of this scale generated significant momentum and motivation for our team.

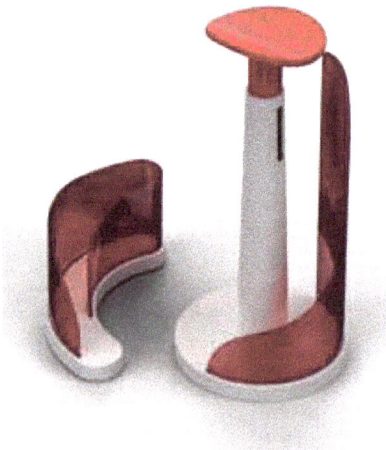

WHICH SECTORS DO YOU WORK FOR? DO YOU HAVE A PREFERENCE?

Altera Design Studio is a multidisciplinary design firm, focusing on product, activity and space design. We work for firms in various sectors. We reconfigure the design process, from the concept stage to the production stage, according to the needs of each sector. In addition to our intensive work in the Lighting, Home and Office Furniture, Furniture Accessories, Building Components and Medical sectors, we occasionally design for Kitchen Utensils, Toys and Packaging sectors. Arlight, Heper Group, Lamp83, Üzümcü Medical, Çebi Kilit, Hakart, Çetin Plastik, Procter&Gamble, Fy Mobilya, Işık Oyuncak, Star Plastik and Duş'al are among the firms for which we provide design and consulting services.

In terms of sectors, I could say that the lighting sector is where we get the highest demand for our services.

CAN YOU TELL US ABOUT YOUR ONGOING PROJECTS?

Right now we are working on two lighting product design projects simultaneously. One of them is a LED street lighting fixture for Arlight and the other is a spotlight product family for Lamp83. We are a multidisciplinary design office and we also work on activity and space design. We recently completed the activity design of a mobile tent for Prima. We are still working on their

booth design for the Mother Baby Child Fair that will be held in January 2016.

In addition to offering design and consulting services to firms, we recently started to get our own products manufactured. Tea, tea glasses and trays are traditional elements of Anatolian culture, which we reinterpreted with contemporary concepts such as speed, user friendliness and sustainability, and created Spring. The production of this set will start in February 2016 and it will be displayed at the Ambiente Fair 2016.

WHAT DO YOU THINK OF TURKEY'S POSITION IN THE INDUSTRIAL DESIGN SECTOR AND ESPECIALLY IN THE KITCHEN UTENSILS SEGMENT?

The culture of design is still at its infancy in Turkey, not only in the kitchen utensils sector but in all industries. Of course there are pioneering firms that manage to establish this awareness, employ in-house designers and/or acquire design services. The question is how to create this awareness about the added-value of working with designers in other producers.

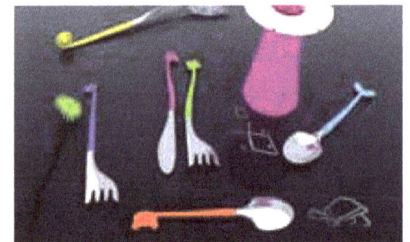

MERİÇ KARA

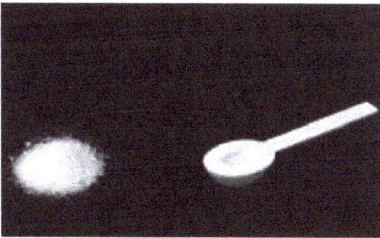

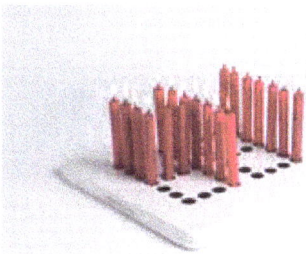

"IN TURKEY WE CAN SEE ORIGINAL WORKS"

MERİÇ KARA SAYS, "WE HAVE DESIGNERS AND COMPANIES THAT HAVE A VERY GOOD MASTERY OF THE KITCHEN. SOME LARGE FIRMS HAVE BEGUN TO DEVELOP SPECIAL COLLECTIONS WITH DESIGNERS."

We came to know designer Meriç Kara, who says "I am interested in all areas where concept takes center stage, where the material's potential can be used," and we spoke with him about the world of design.

WHO IS MERİÇ KARA, AND HOW DID SHE STEP INTO THE WORLD OF DESIGN?

I was born in 1977, in İzmir. I earned my Bachelor's Degree in Industrial Products Design at METU in 2001, and earned my postgraduate degree with honors at the Domus Academy in Milan in 2002. I was part of the Design Department at Benetton's Communication and Research Center Fabrica in Italy between 2003 and 2005, and collaborated with designers such as Jaime Hayon and Aldo Cibic during this period. My works have been featured in various international exhibitions, fairs, publications, and companies since 2003. I founded Meriç Kara Tasarım ve Danışmanlık in Istanbul in 2009. I opened my first solo exhibit in 2010, and was elected "young designer of the year" by the Elle Décor magazine with this work. I began working as design editor for Size Magazine in 2011. I began teaching part time at the Bilgi University School of Architecture in 2012.

WHAT SECTORS DO YOU DESIGN FOR? WHAT IS YOUR PARTICULAR FIELD OF CHOICE?

I work in various areas since the idea takes center stage in my work. I take part in joint projects with architects and advertising firms, and sometimes implement my own designs. I also take part in exhibits where I can interpret products. I design promotional products, indoor installations, serial and custom industrial productions, household and office objects. I am interested in all areas from notebooks to kitchen wares, where the concept takes center stage, where the potential of the material can be used, by trying and researching over and over.

WOULD YOU GIVE US INFORMATION ABOUT YOUR CURRENT WORK?

I have most recently designed various bags for a corporate firm; we have designed an iPad cover, a pencil box, and cylindrical containers etc. products for architects in felt. I am currently working on new designs in this area. I am developing the ideas I had liked, but that had stayed as sketches under my own brand.

WHERE DO YOU THINK TURKEY IS IN TERMS OF INDUSTRIAL DESIGN PARTICULARLY IN KITCHENWARE?

We have designers and companies that have a very good mastery of the kitchen. Some large firms have begun to develop special collections with designers, and to promote designers along with the exhibition, by also accentuating designer's names. Competitions related to the subject have also begun to increase. We can see original works. I hope similar approaches will be possible in other firms as well, as soon as possible. As companies come together with designers with whom they are compatible, more products will emerge that distinguish brand identity, are focused, speak the same language, and increase each other's strength.

"THERE IS AN INTEREST IN DESIGN, AND THERE WILL ALWAYS BE"

SEYMAN ÇAY

STATING THAT THERE IS AN EVER INCREASING NUMBER OF COMPANIES ACQUIRING DESIGN SERVICES, "THERE IS AN INTEREST IN DESIGN, AND THERE WILL ALWAYS BE," SAYS SEYMAN ÇAY.

We had an interview for Turkish Kitchenware with Seyman Çay who is currently creating his design work under MG Design.

WHO IS SEYMAN ÇAY, AND HOW DID HE STEP INTO THE WORLD OF DESIGN?

I graduated from the Industrial Product Design program of Istanbul Technical University. I currently attend workshop classes as a visiting scholar at the same university. I am also the design executive at MG Design. We are striving to maintain customer satisfaction at the highest level by adding and improving new industrial design methods to the ones that can otherwise be called "classical" back in the years we have started our journey at MG Design. We have a design approach in MG Design. We believe in a lean product language. We make each decision based upon a reason. In doing so we isolate design from non-functional elements, which leads to the emergence of self-explanatory products.

WHAT SECTORS DO YOU DESIGN FOR?

We provide services in various fields such as consumer products, domestic appliances, electric kitchen tools, power tools, laser products, electrical and electronic products, sanitary ware, sports equipments and accessories, product design for the companies engaged in different industries such as packaging, developing design language, GUI - interface design, product conceptualization, building prototypes, and concept research projects.

WHAT IS THE POSITION OF TURKEY IN DESIGN?

There is an interest in design, and there will always be. Despite the fact that the number of companies that acquire design services are fairly high, there is a large part of companies that have not yet built that kind of collaboration in terms of percentage. The main threshold for resistance for the companies that will procure services for the first time is the beginning. However this resistance be overcome by a bit of courage and allocating time. Industrial design in a sense, as well as all the other creative industries, provides imagination and promises success. One should remember though, sometimes it all starts with a dream. What is important after that stage is choosing the right solution partners. It is difficult to evaluate industrial design in global scale. We compete in three main areas: cost, quality, and design.

avsar
since 1982
ceramic & non-stick & enamel

AMBIENTE FAIR
HALL 3.0 A90

PorSteel

www.avsar.com

BURCU BÜYÜKÜNAL

SHE BOTH DESIGNS,
AND PRODUCES

INDUSTRIAL DESIGNER BURCU BUYUKUNAL WHOSE PRINCIPAL AREA OF DESIGN IS JEWELRY HAS MOST RECENTLY DESIGNED TEA GLASSES AND DECORATIVE BOWLS FOR THE PAŞABAHÇE OMNIA COLLECTION.

We spoke with Burcu Büyükünal who is in the process of preparing for her March exhibit about her designs.

WHO IS BURCU BÜYÜKÜNAL?

I graduated from the Industrial Product Design program of ITU. After my graduation I began working with Ela Cindoruk and Nazan Pak's jewelry workshop. During the four years I worked there I both designed and produced. Then I won the Fulbright Scholarship and earned my postgraduate degree in the Metal program of the State University of New York at New Paltz.

HOW DID YOU STEP INTO THE WORLD OF DESIGN?

Soon after returning to Turkey I worked for Özlem Tuna for a brief period where I designed decorative bowls, espresso and coffee cups in addition to jewelry. In 2011, I founded the Maden Çağdaş Mücevher Atölyesi with my partner Selen Özus, and

continue my work with my production in the area of contemporary jewelry and the training we provide on this subject. My most current work over the recent period are the tea glasses and decorative bowls I designed for Paşabahçe's Omnia Collection. This was also a return to industrial product design for me.

WHAT SECTORS DO YOU DESIGN FOR? WHAT IS YOUR PARTICULAR FIELD OF CHOICE?

I particularly work in the area of contemporary jewelry at the moment. I like working in this field.

WOULD YOU GIVE US INFORMATION ABOUT YOUR CURRENT WORK?

I am currently working for the

contemporary jewelry exhibit I will open in March. Since it will be new work I do not wish to give out much information, but it has been a different approach than my previous work. I usually design and produce in the form of series. This job includes series as well but will also include individual works I have created.

avşar
ceramic & non-stick & enamel
since 1982

**AMBIENTE FAIR
HALL 3.0 A90**

www.avsar.com

Style

AMBIENTE'S STAR PRODUCTS

FOR OUR SPECIAL AMBIENTE ISSUE, WE HAVE ONCE AGAIN CHOSEN FOR YOU PRODUCTS THAT ARE EXCELLENT FROM COLOR TO PATTERN, MATERIAL TO QUALITY, PRODUCTS YOU WILL USE FOR MANY YEARS. YOU WILL BE ABLE TO THESE PRODUCTS ALL OF WHICH HAVE BEEN MANUFACTURED IN TURKEY WITH CONFIDENCE IN YOUR

Stainless steel pots **Özkent**
Cake container **Göreme Melamin**
Cam şişe ve sürahiler **Renga**
Cornflakes serving tool **Zicco**
Cast iron grill and toaster **Lava**
Jar with silicon gate **Zucci**
Ceramic pots **Hascevher**
Dish, salt and pepper shakers **Obje Plastik**
Bucket kit and napkin holder **Lux Plastic**
Salad bowls **Gondol Plastik**

Markiz dinner set **Emsan**

Cornflakes serving tool **Zicce**

Granite pots and pans
Hascevher

Stainless steel pressure cooker
Ayyıldız Export

Food container **Zucci**

Porcelain dinnerware **Porland**

Glass bottles
Renga

Glass bowl **PlusKitchen**

sty

Cast iron pan **Lava**

Grater **Obje Plastik**

Stainless steel pots **Korkmaz**

Enamel pots **Luyano**

Food container **Lux Plastic**

Rustica dinner set **Emsan**

Spoons **Nehir**

Bohem dinner set **Porland**

turkish
kitchen
ware

style

Olimpos dinner set
Kütahya Porselen

Food containert **Gondol Plasti**

Enamel tableware **Luyano**

Salad bowl **Lux Plastic**

Papilla®

"passion of cooking"

AMBIENTE (Germany)
Hall: 3
Stand: H-50
12-16 Fubruary 2016

IHHS 2016 CHICAGO (USA)
Hall & Stand: S4370
5-8 March 2016

Granito Technology

Wilma Series

www.papilla.com.tr

Head office: Istoc 16. Ada Sonu, Aslan Plaza, Kat :4 34218 Bağcılar Istanbul-Turkiye
Tel: +90 212 676 7838 **Fax:** +90 212 676 7839
email: info@papilla.com.tr

Factory: E-5 Karayolu Uzeri, Akmese, Kartepe, Uzunciftlik Izmit - Turkiye
Tel: +90 262 371 3248 **Fax:** +90 262 371 3247
www.papilla.com.tr

ADEM ATMACA, MEMBER OF THE JUMBO EXECUTIVE BOARD STATES THAT THEIR AGENDA FOR 2016 INCLUDED OPENING NEW STORES AND INCREASING THE NUMBER OF THEIR SALES POINTS, AND SAYS THEY AIM TO REACH 50 STORES BY THE END OF THE YEAR. ATMACA ADDS, "THE MOVEMENT IN OUR COLLECTIONS WILL OF COURSE CONTINUE WITH INCREASED SPEED. INNOVATIONS NEVER END AT JUMBO, IN 2016 TOO..."

"INNOVATIONS NEVER END AT JUMBO"

We heard the story of Jumbo which has brought countless awards to Turkey with fine workmanship that gives life sot steel, porcelain, glass, and stone and over 120 industrial designs from Adem Atmaca, member of its Executive Board.

WOULD YOU BRIEFLY TELL US OF THE FOUNDING OF JUMBO?

The story of Jumbo begins in a workshop in Çemberlitaş, Istanbul. Since its founding, it has been a leading organization which has signed its name on all stages of development of the market. Jumbo which began production by making spoons of cast yellow metal achieves European standards by using the technology of tin coating on DKP (Decoupaged sheet metal) with the presses and rolling equipment added to its workshop during the 1950's. The manufacturing of stainless steel forks, spoons, and unbreakable knives also commence during these years. The recognition which begins in the 1950's is transformed into a rapid process of branding during the 1960's. During the 1980's Jumbo acquires a lifetime guarantee certificate for its products, becoming the first company to establish after sales service. The fruits of all these labors came with design awards during the 2000's. In the beginning of 2014 Jumbo entered a restructuring process, and we are working with all our might to advance our brand even further. For people who wish to distinguish themselves for their choices, we want quality in design to be associated with Jumbo today, as it was yesterday. Jumbo must always be the first address for those seeking timeless designs.

HOW DID YOU DEVELOP JUMBO'S BRAND CREATION PROCESS AND RECOGNITION? WHAT KIND OF INVESTMENTS HAVE YOU MADE TO DATE IN CREATING THE BRAND?

Having achieved firsts such as the first stainless steel fork, stainless steel spoon, unbreakable knife, and modern collection production in Turkey, Jumbo brought a rich breath to its designs and collections during the 2000's. Since the day of its founding Jumbo has been a brand which has carried outs its production without compromising durability and quality, and above world standards, and guided its sector with its designs. It reinforced its image of quality with aesthetics during the 1980's and with the qualities of design, registration, and availability during the 90's. The point reached during the 2000's was the power to determine the fashion trends of the sector. Jumbo has brought countless awards to Turkey with fine workmanship that gives life sot steel, porcelain, glass, and stone and over 120 industrial designs. Jumbo has grown with our belief in innovation and creativity throughout the years, and managed to be listed among the most reliable brands.

WHAT KIND OF COLLABORATION DO YOU HAVE WITH LOCAL OR FOREIGN INVESTORS AS YOU DESIGN YOUR PRODUCTS?

Jumbo gets its design philosophy from nature and from people. It ascribes importance to the aesthetic and design dimension of products, in addition to their intended purpose. Each Jumbo product is very special and valuable. Therefore we try to reflect our design philosophy in every product. For this purpose, we always have projects which we want to implement with both local and foreign designers. Going on inter-cultural voyages is among Jumbo's plans. We will expedite these projects as our store opening efforts progress.

WHAT DO YOUR PLANS FOR THE FUTURE ENTAIL?

Our 2016 agenda primarily includes opening new stores and increasing the number of our sales points. We aim to reach 50 stores by the end of the year. The movement in our collections will of course continue with increased speed. Innovations never end at Jumbo, in 2016 too…

ADEM ATMACA
MEMBER OF THE JUMBO
EXECUTIVE BOARD

HOW DO YOU CREATE THE PRODUCTS OF THE NEW SEASON? WHAT INSPIRES THE DETAILS AND LINES IN THE DESIGNS, THE CONCEPTS CREATED?

Jumbo considers design an essential point for Jumbo, influences its sector accordingly. Therefore we are working to see further ahead than everyone else, to think differently, and to inspire our customers, and try to produce timeless designs. Products manufactured of stainless steel are shaped with the precision and care of a jewelry designer. Jumbo models are manufactured primarily for homes and specially for all types of environments and climates such as restaurants, hotels, holiday resorts, boats, and summer homes.

In addition to product design, Jumbo exercises great care in the design of packaging and boxes for the storage, display, or gifting of products. We know that our customer exercises the same care after purchasing our products as we have while designing them. We act on this awareness.

WOULD YOU GIVE US INFORMATION ABOUT THE WEIGHT OF JUMBO IN THE SECTOR AND WHAT SHARE OF ITS PRODUCTION IS SOLD WITHIN THE COUNTRY AND OVERSEAS?

We naturally have both local and overseas connections. The essential point

for Jumbo in making the decision to manufacture is to be positioned where there is quality. We follow masterful workmanship and proceed with quality we can sign our name on.

WOULD YOU TELL US BRIEFLY OF YOUR PRODUCT VARIETIES?

We carry the Jumbo quality and signature well known in cutlery to bone dining sets. These days, the product portfolio in our stores is constantly renewed. Our claim is to offer a full table set only with Jumbo! Aside from this, we exist in kitchen and food preparation group products with our stainless steel quality. Our products manufactured of genuine granite that have recently joined the cooking group are the first and only examples of their kind in Turkey. Natural granite products retain more speed than conventional pans, and preserve all the nutritional value and flavor of the food by giving this heat back gradually. Thus, the journey which begins in the kitchen preserves its flavor with in all its warmth on your table as well. In the future, we wish products bearing the signature of Jumbo, the symbol of quality and design will not to be confined to tables and kitchens, but take their places in various corners of the home with original pieces reflecting the line of Jumbo.

THE INDISPENSABLE OLD CRAFT OF THE TURKISH KITCHEN: TINSMITHING

THE PROFESSION OF TINSMITHING, WHICH DATES BACK TO 3000 B.C. AND IS KNOWN AS PART OF THE TURKISH CULTURE, IS ON THE VERGE OF OBLIVION. ALUMINUM ALLOY STAINLESS KITCHEN WARE EMERGES IN THE 1960'S, WHICH LED TO THE DECLINE OF THE TINSMITH'S PROFESSION, WHICH HAS NEARLY DISAPPEARED TODAY.

insmithing, a part of Turkish culture is falling into oblivion. Tinsmiths of which there are only a few in cities say the profession will soon be eradicated, since there are no apprentices learning the craft. The profession of tinsmithing, which dates back to 3000 B.C. and is known as part of the Turkish culture, is on the verge of oblivion.

As is known, copper kitchen pots must be tinned since they become toxic as their coating dissolves in time. For this reason, tinsmiths, and the craft of tinsmithing used to be popular until about 20 years ago. With advancing technology, copper pots and pans were replaced with chrome, steel,

WHERE IS IT CARRIED OUT?

Tinsmithing is developed everywhere there is coppersmithing. Tinsmith's shops can be infrequently encountered in some big cities such as Istanbul, Ankara, İzmir, Gaziantep, Diyarbakır, and Trabzon as well as in some districts such as Beypazarı, Ayaş, and Tire where traditional crafts still survive. Today, tin is mined in 35 countries including Malaysia, Bolivia, Thailand, Indonesia, Nigeria, and China. The oldest known tin mine in Anatolia is in Niğde. Tin mines exist in Tunceli, Kırklareli, Tekirdağ, Istanbul-Şile, Eskişehir, Bursa, Manisa, Kırşehir, Amasya, Uşak, Niğde, Sivas, and Aksaray.

and aluminum alloy kitchen wares. There used to be traveling tinsmiths as well. Tinsmiths who used to go from village to village, neighborhood to neighborhood with their hand barrows and their horse drawn wagons were eventually confined to shops in remote corners of cities.

TINSMITHING IS A PART OF TURKISH CULTURE

Tinsmiths say that tinning which used to be carried out over a wood or coal fire began to be done over an LPG fire with advancing technology. Copper kitchen pots and pans have now become historical items. Such items are viewed as antiques, and used for decorative purposes after being tinned.

Tinsmithing is also recorded in sources as being a part of Turkish culture. Old Turks used to go about their lives by fulfilling all of their needs with their own skills. Tinsmithing used to be one of these skills. Turks took care to cook their food in tinned bowls,

fermented their yoghurt in tinned pots, and cooked their wedding feasts in tinned basins and cauldrons.

MULTIPLE STAGES

There are quite interesting keys to tinning. First, the pot that is to be tinned is repaired using a hammer and anvil to get rid of any irregularities. Crushed parts are evened out, any cracks are welded. These pots are later cleaned using sand and pieces of

coal by the tinner's apprentice. Any darkened parts are rubbed until they once again gleam. Fine sand, and pieces of coal are placed on the pot, and a piece of burlap is laid on these pieces. The pot is rubbed clean using these. This was sanding in a time where there was no sandpaper. The bellows must be rotated to flare up the fire in the hearth. Aside from single and double handled leather bellows, there are also bellows that are ventilators, with hand driven iron blades.

The pot thus cleaned is heated over the hearth. Salammoniac powder is sprinkled on the heated pot, to ensure adhesion of the tin. A small portion of tin is brought into contact with the heated container sprinkled with salammoniac. The tin is now melted on the pot. The liquid tin is spread evenly around the pot, using a wad of cotton. This is repeated until the pot is fully coated with tin, and the tinning is complete when the pot has cooled down.

TURKISH HOUSEWARES UR-GE PROJECT TRAINING

The need analysis, the first stage of the Turkish Housewares UR-GE (Support of the Development of International Competition) project held for the benefit of the household and kitchen wares sector by the Istanbul Chemicals and Chemical Products Exporters' Association (İKMİB), in collaboration with the Home and Kitchen Appliances Industrialists and Exporters Association (EVSİD) was completed with the reception of the Ministry of Finance's approval. The training arranged within the scope of the project for the benefit of cluster firms, the "Getting Maximum Efficiency from Bilateral Business Meetings" was provided by Ekol Drama and took place at the Foreign Trade Complex with a duration of 2 days on December 3-4, and December 10-11.

2. TURKISH KITCHENWARE CLUSTER

The need analysis was carried out by visits to 23 firms, within the scope of the "2nd Kitchen and Houseware" Ur-Ge (Support of the Development of International Competition) Project Need Analysis that had been implemented with the coordinatorship of the Istanbul Ferrous & Non Ferrous Metals Exporters' Association (İDDMİB), with ZÜCDER (Turkish Glassware Association) as a project partner. With this need analysis, the cluster's consulting needs, strategy, and target markets were determined. The training events specified in the need analysis will be followed with local and overseas marketing events.

During the "Needs Analysis Closing Meeting" that will be held after the completion of the need analysis stage, works will be shared on the basis of companies and the cluster, and the roadmap for the 3 year project will be determined. The cluster activities

THE TURKISH HORECA CLUSTER

The sector showed great interest in the Industrial Kitchen UR-GE project that had been announced during the past months, and that will be conducted by İDDMİB and TÜSİD (Laundry and Catering Equipment Manufacturers' and Distributors' Association) in partnership, and 48 companies participated in the project. The first stage of the project, need analysis, will be carried out in January and February and the cluster will begin operations expeditiously

that will begin with training in 2016 are planned to continue with local and overseas marketing visits and fair participations.

İMMİB TAKES THE SCENE AT AMBIENTE WITH 71 FIRMS

The Ambiente fair, held annually as the world's largest fair in the kitchen and house wares sectors is held between February 12 and 16, 2016, once again with high attendance of Turkish firms. The national participation in the Ambiente 2016 fair, where Turkish firms participating in the fair on an individual basis also meet visitors and participants from all around the world is organized by İMMİB.

Aside from individual participants, İMMİB participates in the Ambiente fair, in which Turkey has participated on a national scale for the 21st time, in halls 3.0, 5.0, and 10.1, taking the scene with 71 firms. Turkish firms which offer a wide product range including metal kitchenware, small electrical appliances, plastic kitchen and house wares, glass items, yard furniture and gift items draw the attention of purchasers with their competitive prices and superior quality products.

We invite you readers, to the

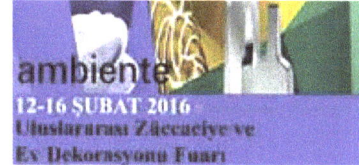

Turkish national booths to get information on Turkish brands. Through other sector reports and lists of manufacturing firms, you will have the chance to access not all firms at the fair, but also all firms in the sector.

WE HAVE MADE A TRADE DELEGATION VISIT TO THE USA

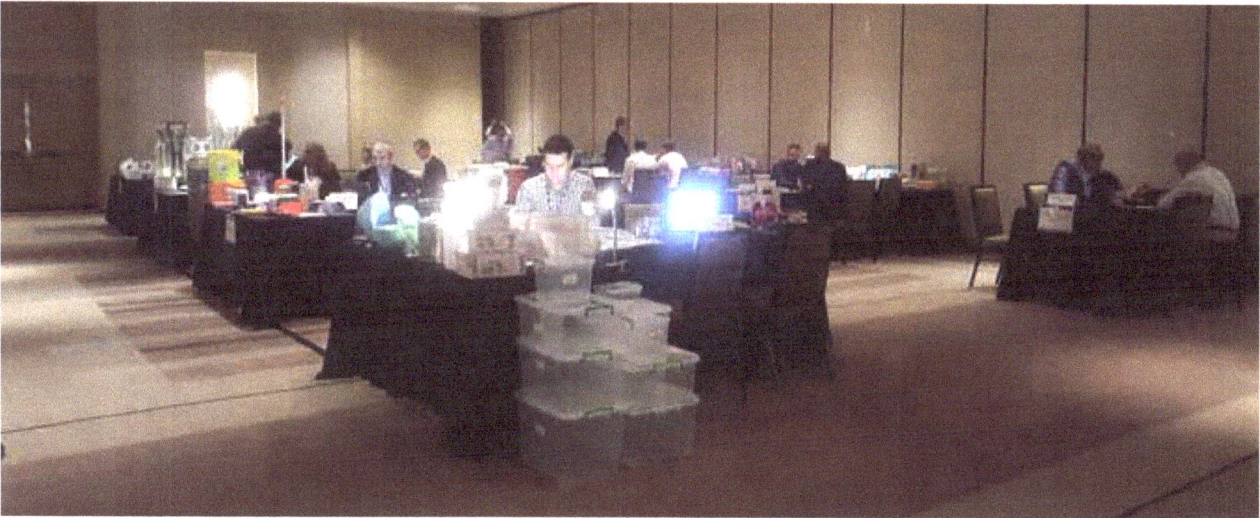

Within the scope of the events held for the benefit of the Turkish house and kitchen wares sector, a sub-sector of the Chemical Products Exporters' Association (İKMİB), a sectoral commercial delegation visit was held to Fort Lauderdale/USA between the 25th and 29th of October, 2015 with the attendance of 9 companies from the sector in question. Each company had an average of 30 meetings during the two day one-on-one business meetings event. The delegation was joined by Recep Aslan, Head of the Office of the General Directorate of Exports of the Ministry of Finance, and stated is opinion that the ECRM one-on-one business meetings were very beneficial for companies.

AWARDS OF THE 2ND PLASTIC AND METAL PACKAGING DESIGN COMPETITION WERE HANDED OUT

The second instance of the Plastic and Metal Packaging Design Competition, that had been implemented for the purpose of offering export products to world markets with original and innovative packaging designs, was held. Competitors who earned rankings in the Professional and Student branches of the Plastic and Metal categories received awards amounting to TRY 110 thousand in total. Winners who ranked first in the competition also earned the chance to visit prestigious packaging fairs overseas, and to use the Ministry of Finance's overseas education scholarship.

The Plastic and Metal Packaging Design Competition held by collaboration between the Chemical

Products Exporters' Association (İKMİB) and the Istanbul Ferrous & Non Ferrous Metals Exporters' Association (İDDMİB) received 201 Professional and Student applications in two categories. This year, highly creative ideas were put forward in the Plastic and Metal Packaging Design Competition which aims to gain new designers for the packaging sector that has a global magnitude of 700 billion dollars and has reached a magnitude of 20 billion dollars in our country, and to encourage companies to invest in design.

In the Professional Category of 'Plastic Packaging', Muharrem Şeyda won first place with its oil packaging design named 'Phoenix' which encourages collection of used oil for recycling, while Yusuf Çağlar won first place in the Student Category with the lamp packaging named 'Light' which can also be used as a droplight. Umut Demirel won first place in the Professional Category of Metal Packaging for his cookie set design named 'Baker' which was striking for its practical and functional design while

Berk Kaplan won first place with his coffee packaging design which allows portioning coffee thanks to its rotating mechanism and brings elegance to kitchens wit its metallic finish.

Ömer Karadeniz, Member of the Executive Board of İKMİB and Packaging Committee Representative gave a speech at the opening of the ceremony where he pointed out that the need for design and branding was rapidly increasing, and stressed that sustainability of export required the ability to remain competitive. Tahsin Öztiryaki, Vice Chairman of the Executive Board of İDDMİB emphasized that they were striving to lay the seeds for design an innovation through the competitions and projects they organized, while creating an environment where information and new ideas collected. Mehmet Büyükekşi, Chairman of the Turkish Exporters' Assembly who attended and gave a speech at the 2nd Plastic and Metal Packaging Design Competition Award Ceremony pointed out the great importance of design in increasing added value in exportation.

CONTACT**FILE**

TURKISH KITCHENWARE EXPORTERS

KITCHENWARE ●

PLASTICWARE ●

ELECTRICAL ●

INDUSTRIAL ●

TABLEWARE ●

GIFTWARE ●

HOUSEWARE ●

FOR MORE INFORMATION ABOUT
TURKISH KITCHENWARE, PLEASE CONTACT US
bugra.erol@immib.org.tr

iMMiB

İSTANBUL MINERAL AND METALS EXPORTERS' ASSOCIATION
Dış Ticaret Kompleksi-A Blok Çobançeşme Mevkii, Sanayi Cad. 34197 Yenibosna Bahçelievler - İstanbul
TURKEY Tel: +90 212 454 00 00 Fax: +90 212 454 00 01 e-mail: immib@immib.org.tr www.immib.org.tr

HOUSEWARE • GIFTWARE • TABLEWARE • INDUSTRIAL • ELECTRICAL • PLASTICWARE • KITCHENWARE

3-D THE GLASSWARE COMPANY
Tel: +90 216 583 04 70 Fax: +90 216 583 04 81
Web: www.3dglassware.com e-mail: info@3dglassware.com

AB-KA KRİSTAL DECORATED GLASSWARE
Tel: +90 216 465 55 15 Fax: +90 216 465 55 14
Web: www.abkakristal.com, e-mail: altan@abkakristal.com

AEB HOTEL EQUIPMENT INC.
Tel: +90 242 322 90 56 Fax: +90 242 322 60 50
Web: www.aebhotelequipments.com,
e-mail: info@aebhotelequipments.com

AHMETAL
Tel: +90 272 612 88 02 Gsm: 009 0532 451 60 82
Web: www.ahmetal.com.tr, e-mail: export@ahmetal.com.tr

AKAY PLASTIC INDUSTRY TRADE INC.
Tel: +90 212 659 11 87 Fax: +90 212 659 11 89
Web: www.akayplastik.com.tr, e-mail: info@akayplastik.com.tr

AKCAM GLASS PLASTIC CONSTRUCTION CO.
Tel: +90 216 378 74 50 Fax: +90 216 378 87 30
Web: www.ak-cam.com.tr, e-mail: export@ak-cam.com.tr

AKDEM MUTFAK GEREÇLERİ ÇELİK SAN. TİC. LTD.ŞTİ
Tel: +90 344 236 34 01 Fax: +90 344 236 34 06
Web: www.akdem.com.tr, e-mail: akdem@akdem.com.tr

AKER ELEKTRİKLİ EV ALETLERİ
Tel: +90 212 876 93 77 Fax: +90 212 876 93 55
Web: www.aker-mutfak.com, e-mail: aker@akerticaret.com

AKSEL KITCHENWARE IND. AND. TRADE
Tel: +90 212 617 12 60 Fax: +90 212 538 22 28
Web: www.akselmutfak.com, e-mail: info@akselmutfak.com.tr

AKYILDIZ MUTFAK EŞYALARI
Tel: +90 344 257 91 88 Fax: +90 344 257 91 87
Web: www.akykitchen.com, e-mail: info@akykitchen.com

AKYOL PLASTİK
Tel: +90 212 550 30 21 Fax: +90 212 550 54 47
Web: www.akyol.com.tr, e-mail: info@akyol.com.tr

AKYÜZ PLASTIC
Tel: +90 212 612 94 00 Fax: +90 212 577 60 92
Web: www.akyuz.com.tr, e-mail: info@akyuz.com.tr

ALBA TURİSTİK VE HEDİYELİK EŞYA
Tel: +90 212 578 87 96 Fax: +90 212 578 87 96
Web: www.albasis.com, e-mail: info@albasis.com

AL-CO ALÜMİNYUM / Papilla
Tel: +90 212 676 78 38 Fax: +90 212 676 78 39
Web: www.alcocookware.com, , www.papilla.com.tr
e-mail: adalgic@alcocookware.com, info@papilla.com.tr

ALBAYRAK MELAMİN PLASTİK
Tel: +90 212 659 33 75 Fax: +90 212 659 33 80
Web: www.albayrakmelamin.com, e-mail: info@albayrakmelamin.com

ALEVLİ ZÜCCACİYE TİCARET A.Ş
Tel: +90 212 219 51 11 Fax: +90 212 225 02 93
Web: www.alevli.com.tr, e-mail: info@alevli.com.tr

ALKAN ZÜCCACİYE SAN. VE TİC. LTD. ŞTİ.
Tel: +90 212 527 15 92 Fax: +90 212 528 13 69
Web: www.alkanzuccaciye.com, e-mail: zicco@alkanzuccaciye.com

ALP PLASTİK KALIP SANAYİ / Moonstar
Tel: +90 212 875 26 66 Fax: +90 212 875 26 46
Web: www.moonstar.com.tr, e-mail: moonstar@moonstar.com.tr

ALPİN STEEL
Tel: +90 212 875 02 22 Fax: +90 212 875 02 26
Web: www.bertone.com.tr, e-mail: info@bertone.com.tr

ALYANS METAL
Tel: +90 344 236 11 65 Fax: +90 344 236 44 25
Web: www.alyansmetal.com.tr, e-mail: info@alyansmetal.com.tr

ANİKYA İZNİK TILE
Tel: +90 216 422 88 41 Fax: +90 216 422 88 43
Web: www.anikya.com, e-mail: info@anikya.com

ANİVA EV URUNLERİ METAL SAN. TİC. LTD. ŞTİ.
Tel: +90 262 751 21 94 Fax: +90 262 751 21 98
Web: www.ayhanmetal.com.tr
e-mail: ayhanmetal@ayhanmetal.com.tr

ANSAN METAL AND PLASTIC
Tel: +90 212 422 05 06 Fax: +90 212 422 85 82
Web: www.ansan.com.tr, e-mail: exp1@ansan.com.tr

ARAS METAL
Tel: +90 212 855 27 80 Fax: +90 212 856 08 26
Web: www.arasmetal.com, e-mail: arasmetal@superonline.com

ARÇELİK
Tel: +90 212 314 34 34 Web: www.arcelik.com.tr
e-mail: melis.mutus@arcelik.com.tr, seher.turkpence@arcelik.com.tr

ARDA GLASSWARE
Tel: +90 212 422 10 66 Fax: +90 212 422 10 71
Web: www.ardaglassware.com
e-mail: contact@ardaglassware.com

ARMA METAL DIS TİC.LTD.ŞTİ.
Tel: +90 344 251 33 00 - Fax: +90 344 251 31 31
Web: www.armametal.com, e-mail: info@armametal.com

ARMADA METAL SANAYİ VE TİCARET LTD. ŞTİ.
Tel: +90 212 694 58 82 - Fax: 212 591 75 54
Web:www.armadametal.com,
e-mail: satis@armadametal.com

ARMONI A.Ş.
Tel: +90 212 798 36 37 Fax: +90 212 798 36 46
Web: www.armonipazarlama.com, e-mail: armoni@armonipazarlama.com

ARTAÇ KITCHENWARE MANUFACTURING COMPANY
Tel: +90 212 798 25 75 Fax: +90 212 798 25 79
Web: www.artac.com.tr, e-mail: info@artac.com.tr

ARTEK ELEKTRİKLİ EV ALETLERİ SAN. VE TİC. LTD. ŞTİ.
Tel: +90 212 256 47 63-64 Fax: +90 212 255 04 90
Web: www.ar-tek.com, e-mail: ar-tek@ar-tek.com

ARTEPELLE HEDİYELİK EŞYA
Tel: +90 212 283 29 30 Fax: +90 212 283 29 21
Web: www.arte-pelle.com, e-mail: info@arte-pelle.com

AR-YILDIZ MADENİ MUTFAK EŞYALARI SAN. TİC. A.Ş.
Tel: +90 282 681 84 60 Fax: +90 282 681 84 70
Web: www.aryildiz.com, e-mail: info@aryildiz.com

ARZU ÇELİK METAL SAN. TİC. LTD. ŞTİ. / Asstarline
Tel: +90 344 236 05 03 Fax: +90 344 236 11 87
Web: www.arzumetal.com.tr, e-mail: export@arzumetal.com

ARZUM SMALL DOMESTIC APPLIANCE / Felix
Tel: +90 212 467 80 80 Fax: +90 212 467 80 00
Web: www.arzum.com.tr, www.felix.com.tr
e-mail: okarahan@arzum.com.tr

AS PLASTIC AND PACKAGING
Tel: +90 216 464 38 48 Fax: +90 216 445 79 02
Web: www.asplastik.com, e-mail: export@asplastik.com

A-SİL KABLO SAN.TİC.VE LTD.ŞTİ
Tel: +90 212 486 02 01 Fax: +90 212 485 00 80
Web: www.casta-sil.com, e-mail: info@casta-sil.com

ASİL TİCARET VE EV ALETLERİ / Noble Life
Tel: +90 212 659 51 00 Fax: +90 212 659 25 15
Web: www.asilticaret.com.tr, www.noblelife.com.tr
e-mail: asil@asilticaret.com.tr

ASKOM OTEL RESTAURANT EQUIPMENTS
Tel: +90 212 513 29 38 Fax: +90 212 526 58 94
Web: www.askom.com, e-mail: askom@askom.com

ASUDE PLASTİK KALIP SAN.TİC
Tel: +90 212 659 23 12-13 Fax: +90 212 659 23 11
Web: www.asudeplastik.com, e-mail: muhase@asudeplastik.com

ATA DÖKÜM SAN. VE TİC. A.Ş
Tel: +90 222 236 82 26 Fax: +90 222 236 82 31
Web: www.surelgrup.com, www.atadokum.com.tr; www.surelmutfak.com
e-mail: atadokum@atadokum.com.tr

ATLANTİK TÜKETİM MAL.SAN.TİC.LTD.ŞTİ.
Tel: +90 212 494 47 74 Fax: +90 212 494 47 75
Web: www.dose.com.tr, e-mail: pazarlama@dose.com.tr

ATLAS DAYANIKLI TÜKETİM MALLARI
Tel: +90 212 585 34 44 Fax: +90 212 589 16 25
Web: www.atlasdtm.com, e-mail: atlas@atlasdtm.com

ATMACA ELEKTRONİK / Cleaner, Sunny, Woon, Cendix, Axen
Tel: +90 212 412 12 12 Fax: +90 212 412 14 99
Web: www.sunny.com.tr, e-mail: halilorenbas@sunny.com.tr

AVA PLASTİK SANAYİ / Avatherm
Tel: +90 282 747 63 33 Fax: +90 282 747 65 31
Web: www.avaplastik.com, e-mail: avaplastik@avaplastik.com

AVŞAR ENAMEL SAN. TİC. A.Ş. / Avsar, Rataly
Tel: +90 272 612 66 00 Fax: +90 272 611 43 34
Web: www.avsar.com, e-mail: export@avsar.com
export3@avsar.com

AYDIN TURİSTİK HEDİYELİK EŞYA VE DEKORASYON
Tel: +90 212 512 60 63 Fax: +90 212 513 45 16
Web: www.exoticlamp.com.tr, e-mail: exoptic@exoticlamp.com.tr

AYSBERG SOĞUTMA METAL SAN. VE TİC.A.Ş
Tel: +90212 886 78 00 Fax: +90 212 886 64 83
Web: www.oztiryakiler.com.tr, e-mail: aysberg@oztiryakiler.com.tr

AYMAK ENDÜSTRİYEL MUTFAK CİHAZLARI SAN. VE TİC.A.Ş.
Tel: +90 242 258 17 10 Fax: +90 242 258 17 14
Web: www.oztiryakiler.com.tr, e-mail: aymak@oztiryakiler.com.tr

AYPAS ELEKTRONİK SAN. TİC. A.Ş. / Galaxy
Tel: +90 212 659 93 33 Fax: +90 212 659 93 34
Web: www.aypas.com.tr
e-mail: gyorur@aypas.com.tr, galaxy@aypas.com.tr

BAGER PLASTİK SAN.VE TİCARET LTD.ŞTİ.
Tel: +90 212 659 57 30 Fax: +90 212 659 02 75
Web: www.bagerplastik.com, e-mail: info@bagerplastik.com

BANAT FIRÇA VE PLASTİK SANAYİ
Tel: +90 212 289 01 50 Fax: +90 212 289 08 29
Web: www.banat.com, e-mail: satis@banat.com

BAŞAK MAKİNA MUTFAK EŞYALARI
Tel: +90 212 485 24 73 Fax: +90 212 485 24 77
Web: www.basakmakina.com.tr, e-mail: info@basakmakina.com.tr

BAYİNER ELEKTRONİK
Tel: +90 216 415 53 36 Fax: +90 216 415 27 37
Web: www.bayiner.com.tr, e-mail: info@bayiner.com.tr

BAYRAKTAR MADENİ EŞYA SAN. VE TİC. LTD. ŞTİ.
Tel: +90 212 659 78 00 Fax: +90 212 659 78 02
Web: www.bayraktarkitchenware.com
e-mail: istoc@bayraktarkitchenware.com

BAYSAN HEATING AND COOLING SYSTEMS
Tel: +90 212 501 84 83 Fax: +90 212 576 33 81
Web: www.baysanmutfak.com, e-mail: baysan@baysanmutfak.com

BEKO
Tel: +90 212 314 34 34 Fax: +90 212 314 34 50
Web: www.beko.com.tr, e-mail: melis.mutus@arcelik.com.tr

● HOUSEWARE
● GIFTWARE
● TABLEWARE
● INDUSTRIAL
● ELECTRICAL
● PLASTICWARE
● KITCHENWARE

BELIVA INTERNATIONAL
Tel: +90 212 659 80 55 Fax: +90 212 659 80 56
Web: www.akelevaletleri.com, e-mail: info@akelevaletleri.com

BEMSA METAL EŞYA SAN. VE TİC.
Tel: +90 344 236 08 84
Web: www.bemsametal.com, e-mail: info@bemsametal.com

BES METAL EŞYA TURİZM KİMYA SAN. TİC. LTD.ŞTİ.
Tel: +90 262 751 48 69 Fax: +90 262 751 48 22
Web: www.besmetal.com, e-mail: info@besmetal.com

BES PLASTİK SANAYİ
Tel: +90 212 876 36 32 Fax: +90 212 876 36 34
Web: www.besplastik.com, e-mail: info@besplastik.com

BEŞTEPE TUBE PROFILE TRADE CO.
Tel: +90 352 322 04 37 Fax: +90 352 322 04 42
Web: www.bestepe.com.tr, e-mail: info@bestepe.com.tr

BİLAL MUTFAK EŞY. SANAYİ VE TİCARET LTD.ŞTİ.
Tel: +90 422 237 55 33 Fax: +90 422 237 55 31
Web: www.bilal.com.tr
e-mail: info@bilal.com.tr

BİLGE METALSAN ÇELİK VE METAL
Tel: +90 212 612 26 30 Fax: +90 212 612 69 12
Web: www.bilgemetal.com
e-mail: bilgemetal@bilgemetal.com

BKL MAKİNE SANAYİ ve TİCARET LTD.ŞTİ
Tel: +90 212 690 37 20-21
Fax: +90 212 428 39 45
Web: www.bklmakine.com
e-mail: bklmakine@bklmakine.com

BLANCO ÖZTİRYAKİLER MUTFAK DONANIMI SAN.
Tel: +90 212 886 57 13 Fax: +90 212 886 57 21
Web: www.blanco.com.tr
e-mail: nadirerbil@blanco.com.tr

BLUE HOUSE-TARMAN DIŞ TİCARET A.Ş.
Tel: +90 212 365 44 44 Pbx Fax: +90 212 365 44 55
Web: www.blue-house.com.tr, e-mail: info@tarmangroup.com

BOĞAZİÇİ INDUSTRIAL
Tel: +90 212 294 22 15 Fax: +90 212 294 97 18
Web: www.bogazicimakina.com, e-mail: bogazici@bogazicimakina.com

BORA PLASTİK SAN. VE TİC. A.Ş.
Tel: +90 212 422 18 50 Fax: +90 212 422 44 34
Web: www.boraplastik.com.tr, e-mail: info@boraplastik.com.tr

BOSCH AND SIEMENS HOME APPLIANCES GROUP
Tel: +90 282 748 30 00 Fax: + 90 282 726 53 96
Web: www.bosch-home.com, e-mail: kurumsaliletisim@bshg.com

BOZTEPE - MEGA STAINLESS STEEL
Tel: +90 258 251 69 90 Fax: +90 258 251 66 10
Web: www.boztepe.com, e-mail: info@boztepe.com

BURÇAK PLASTIC COMPANY
Tel: +90 212 674 75 75 Fax: +90 212 577 77 95
Web: www.burcakplast.com.tr
e-mail: info@burcakplast.com.tr

BURSEV PLASTIC&FOREIGN TRADE
Tel: +90 212 659 06 91 Fax: +90 212 659 06 97
Web: www.bursev.com, e-mail: info@bursev.com

BUTANSAN HOMEWARE
Tel: +90 352 322 00 90 Fax: +90 352 322 00 99
Web: www.butansan.com.tr, e-mail: butansan@hotmail.com.tr

CAMBRO ÖZAY PLASTİK / Ozay, Cambro
Tel: +90 262 751 29 40 Fax: +90 262 751 18 79
Web: www.ozaytray.com, e-mail: ozaytray@ozaytray.com

CAN CAN JUICERS AND KITCHEN EQUIPMENTS
Tel: +90 264 291 49 44 Fax: +90 264 291 49 45
Web: www.cancan.com.tr, www.cancanmakina.com.tr
e-mail: info@cancanmakina.com

CANBA
Tel: +90 212 325 94 13 Fax: +90 212 325 94 12
Web: www.canba.com.tr, e-mail: info@canba.com.tr

CAPRI INDUSTRIAL COOLING & KITCHEN
Tel: +90 224 484 31 15 Fax: +90 224 484 31 17
Web: www.capri.com.tr, e-mail: capri@capri.com.tr

CEM BİALETTİ EV VE MUTFAK EŞYALARI / Cem
Tel: +90 216 445 53 73 Fax: +90 216 445 53 74
Web: www.cembialetti.com
e-mail: info@cembialetti.com

CEMİLE DIŞ TİC. LTD.ŞTİ.
Tel: +90 212 249 91 34 - +90 212 251 58 16
Fax: +90 212 249 91 76
Web: www.cemile.com.tr, e-mail: cemile@cemile.com.tr

CENK METAL - ZEST COOKWARES
Tel: +90 212 567 24 56 Fax: +90 212 544 59 39
Web: www.cenkmetal.com
e-mail: info@cenkmetal.com

ÇELİKAY INDUSTRIAL
Tel: +90 312 319 08 09 Fax: +90 312 319 20 60
Web: www.celikay.com.tr, e-mail: celikay@celikay.com.tr

ÇETİN PLASTİK KALIP SAN.VE TİC.LTD.ŞTİ.
Tel: +90 212 537 48 48 fax: +90 212 537 30 29
Web:www.cetinplastik.com.tr
e-mail:Office@cetinplastik.com.tr
mdeniz@cetinplastik.com.tr

ÇETİN PLASTİK SAN. TİC.LTD.ŞTİ.
Tel: +90 212 502 21 28
Web:www.cetinplastik.com
e-mail:ugur.ozkan@cetinplastik.com

ÇETİNTAŞ BEYAZ EŞYA
Tel: +90 222 236 00 55 Fax: +90 222 235 05 75
Web: www.cetintasbeyazesya.com
e-mail: export@cetintasbeyazesya.com

ÇÖZÜM MUTFAK SAN. VE TİC. A.Ş.
Tel: +90 232 376 72 76 Fax: +90 232 376 72 78
Web: www.cozummutfak.com, e-mail: izmirsts@cozummutfak.com

DALGIÇ GÜMÜŞ SAN. VE DIŞ TİC. LTD. ŞTİ.
Tel: +90 212 482 42 00 Fax: +90 212 482 42 18
Web: www.dalgic.com.tr, e-mail: dalgic@dalgic.com.tr

DAY-CO METAL
Tel: +90 212 493 51 62 Fax: +90 212 493 51 38
Web: www.day-cometal.com, e-mail: info@day-cometal.com

DECORIUM/AR-ŞAH KRİSTAL
Tel: +90 216 595 18 63 Fax: +90 216 378 53 51
Web: www.decorium.com.tr
e-mail: info@decorium.com.tr

DEKOR AHŞAP ÜRÜNLERİ SAN. A.Ş.
Tel: +90 262 678 65 00 Fax: +90 262 642 56 85
Web: www.lineadecor.com.tr
e-mail: export@lineadecor.com.tr,
nazan.kartal@lineadecor.com.tr

DEKOR GLASSWARE FOREIGN TRADE CO.
Tel: +90 212 422 17 01 Fax: +90 212 422 79 73
Web: www.dekorcam.com.tr, e-mail: export@dekorcam.com.tr

DEMİREL PLASTİK VE KALIP SANAYİ
Tel: +90 212 659 59 21 Fax: + 90 212 659 59 23
Web: www.demirelplastik.com, Web: export@demirelplastik.com

DENGE GIDA ÜRÜNLERİ ELEKTRİK ELEK. DAN. VE PAZ.
Tel: +90 212 576 82 81 Fax: +90 212 577 71 17
Web: www.denge-ltd.com.tr, e-mail: info@denge-ltd.com.tr

DENİZLİ CAM SAN. VE TİC. A.Ş.
Tel: +90 212 377 27 65 Fax: +90 212 350 42 73
Web: www.denizlicam.com.tr

DERİA DERİ SANAYİ
Tel: +90 216 573 46 58 Fax: +90 216 573 46 58
Web: www.deria.com.tr, e-mail: ugur@deria.com.tr

DESİNG ZONE GALLERY
Tel: +90 212 527 92 85
Web:www.ozlemtuna.com, e-mail:info@ozlemtuna.com

DİBEKSAN MET. MAT. İHR. İTH. SAN. TİC. LTD. ŞTİ.
Tel: +90 236 313 65 10 Fax: +90 236 314 20 98
Web: www.dibeksan.com, e-mail: dibeksan@dibeksan.com

DİKTAŞ INC. CO.
Tel: +90 312 267 01 90 Fax: +90 312 267 10 03 Web: www.diktas.com,
e-mail: diktas@diktas.com, export1@diktas.com

DİZDAR STAINLESS STEEL KITCHEN EQUIPMENT CO.
Tel: +90 212 444 20 98 Fax: +90 212 690 12 57
Web: www.dizdarsteel.com, e-mail: info@dizdarsteel.com

DKR-DEKOR BANYO
Tel: +90 216 466 56 83 Fax: +90 216 527 53 82
Web: www.dekorbanyo.com, e-mail: info@dekorbanyo.com

DMR SEDEFÇİLİK
Tel: +0506 547 02 03 - 0539 324 23 76
Web: www.dmrsedefcilik.com.tr, e-mail: mozaiksedefkakma@gmail.com

DOĞRULAR MADENİ EŞYA PAZ. LTD. ŞTİ.
Tel: +90 332 239 16 40 Fax: +90 332 239 16 49
Web: www.dogrular.com.tr, e-mail: emin@dogrular.com.tr
mahir@dogrular.com.tr

DOLPHİN ÇÖKERTME CAM SANAYİ
Tel: +90 216 631 66 32 Fax: +90 216 632 19 32
Web: www.dolphinglass.com.tr, e-mail: info@dolphinglass.com.tr

DÜNYA PLASTİK SAN.
Tel: +90 212 489 04 14 Fax: +90 212 489 16 11
Web: www.dunyaplastik.com, e-mail: export@dunyaplastik.com

ECE METAL SAN. VE TİC. LTD. ŞTİ.
Tel: +90 212 481 83 17 Fax: +90 212 481 82 50
Web: www.ecemetal.com.tr, e-mail: info@ecemetal.com.tr

EFBA DAYANIKLI TÜK. MAL. SAN.
Tel: +90 212 486 38 20 Fax: +90 212 486 38 42
Web: www.efba.com.tr, e-mail: info@efba.com.tr

EFE CAM SAN. İTH. İHR.
Tel: +90 212 479 51 51 Fax: +90 212 477 27 88
Web: www.efecam.com.tr, e-mail: export@efecam.com.tr

EFEM MUTFAK
Tel: +90 212 591 20 22 Fax: +90 212 591 60 22
Web: www.efemmutfak.com, e-mail: info@efemmutfak.com

EFES HEDİYELİK EŞYA SAN.
Tel: +90 212 511 30 37 Fax: +90 212 514 59 40
Web: www.colorlightscollection.com, e-mail: info@mosaiclampstore.com

EGE EV ÜRÜNLERİ MADENİ EŞYA PAZARLAMA SAN. VE TİC. LTD. ŞTİ.
Tel: +90 232 853 73 80 Fax: +90 232 853 70 05
Web: www.egeltd.net, e-mail: info@egeltd.net

**EGEMEN HEDİYELİK EŞYA OYUNCAK ZÜCCACİYE ELEK.GIDA
TEKSTİL İNŞ. AMBALAJ SAN. A.Ş.**
Tel: +90 232 437 32 05 Fax: +90 232 437 30 65
Web: www.magicsaverbag.com, e-mail: info@egemen-group.com

EKBER KITCHEN EQUIPMENTS IND.& TRADE CO.
Tel: +90 212 423 92 92 Fax: +90 212 428 17 58
Web: www.ekber.com, e-mail: export@ ekber.com

HOUSEWARE • GIFTWARE • TABLEWARE • INDUSTRIAL • ELECTRICAL • PLASTICWARE • KITCHENWARE

EKONOMA MUTFAK VE SERVİS EKİPMAN SAN. VE TİC. A.Ş.
Tel: +90 212 886 88 00 - 886 88 00 Fax: +90 212 886 68 17
Web: www.oztiryakiler.com.tr, e-mail: ekonoma@oztiryakiler.com.tr

EKSPOPLAST PLASTIC PACKAGING IND.
Tel: +90 216 304 04 24 Fax: +90 216 304 04 29
Web: www.expoplastplastic.com, e-mail: info@expoplastplastic.com

ELEVSAN ELECTRICAL APPLIANCES IND.
Tel: +90 222 236 00 93 Fax: +90 222 236 00 94
Web: www.esco.com.tr, e-mail: export@esco.com.tr

ELİF PLASTİK MUTFAK EŞYALARI
Tel: +90 212 659 22 56 Fax: +90 212 659 56 07
Web: www.elifplastic.com, e-mail: info@elifplastic.com

ELİT FOREIGN TRADE LTD. CO.
Tel: +90 236 237 93 91 Fax: +90 236 238 96 58
Web: www.elitforeigntrade.com, e-mail: info@elitforeigntrade.com
export@elitforeigntrade.com

EMSAN MUTFAK GEREÇLERİ SANAYİ VE TİCARET A.Ş.
Tel: +90 212 495 22 22 Fax: + 90 212 495 45 00
Web: www.emsan.com.tr, Web: info@emsan.com.tr

ENART ENAMEL CO.
Tel: +90 352 321 35 51 Fax: +90 352 321 35 54
Web: www.enartco.com, e-mail: export@enartco.com

ENESCO
Tel: +90 212 520 34 86 Fax: +90 212 520 34 88
Web: www.enescoglass.com, e-mail: info@enescoglass.com

ENKAY ALÜMİNYUM LEVHA MUTFAK EŞYALARI
Tel: +90 362 266 76 26 Fax: +90 362 266 76 27
Web: www.leydimutfak.com, e-mail: leydi@leydimutfak.com

ERA HOME APPLIANCES
Tel: +90 212 407 01 15 – 16 Fax: +90 212 407 01 14
Web: www.eraizgara.com, e-mail: era@eraizgara.com

ERDAL INDUSTRIAL KITCHEN EQUIPMENT
Tel: +90 332 251 51 15 Fax: +90 332 251 51 75
Web: www.erdalmutfak.com.tr,
e-mail: bilgi@erdalmutfak.com.tr

ERDEM KITCHENWARE INDUSTRY
Tel: +90 212 683 22 46 Fax: +90 212 683 22 29
Web: www.erdemkitchen.com, e-mail: ifergan@erdemkitchen.com,
erdem@erdemkitchen.com

ERKOÇ PLASTİK VE KALIP SAN. VE TİC. LTD. ŞTİ.
Tel: +90 212 549 53 85 Fax: +90 212 549 53 87
Web: www.poly-time.com, e-mail: erkoc@poly-time.com

ERNA MAŞ MAKİNA TİC. VE SAN. A.Ş
Tel: +90 212 866 22 00 Fax: +90 212 771 45 00
Web: www.ernamas.com, e-mail: emreg@ernamas.com

ESCO EMAYE DÖKÜM SAN. VE TİC. A.Ş.
Tel: +90 222 236 00 93 Fax: +90 222 236 14 01
Web: www.esco.com.tr, e-mail: export@esco.com.tr

ES-MAK MAKİNE İMALAT SAN.
Tel: +90 212 875 78 16 Fax: +90 212 876 15 33
Web: www.esmak.com.tr, e-mail: mail@esmak.com.tr

ESLON MUTFAK EŞYALARI SAN.VE TİC.LTD.ŞTİ.
Tel: +90 344 257 93 30 Fax: +90 344 257 93 76
Web: www.eslon.com.tr, e-mail: info@eslon.com.tr

ESMER HEDİYELİK
Tel: +90 212 513 76 98 Fax: +90 212 512 17 87
Web: www.esmerbujiteri.com
e-mail: esmer@esmerbujiteri.com

EURO-MEL
Tel: +90 212 486 23 01 Fax: +90 212 486 23 25
Web: www.euro-mel.com,
e-mail: ugur@euro-mel.com, onur@euro-mel.com

EVAS EV ALETLERİ SANAYİ LTD. ŞTİ.
Tel: +90 216 378 73 15 PBX Fax: + 90 216 378 10 06
Web: www.evas.com.tr, e-mail: info@evas.com.tr

EVELİN
Tel: +90 212 659 03 86 Fax: + 90 212 659 03 80
Web: www.evelin.com.tr, e-mail: info@evelin.com.tr

EVREN MUTFAK EŞYALARI SAN.
Tel: +90 212 624 52 21 Fax: +90 212 540 05 00
Web: www.evrenmutfak.com.tr
e-mail: info@evrenmutfak.com.tr

EVREN PLASTİK VE MELAMİN SAN.
Tel: +90 212 550 46 55 Fax: +90 212 550 18 12
Web: www.evrenplastik.com.tr, e-mail: info@evrenplastik.com.tr

EVYELÜKS METAL SAN. TİC. A.Ş.
Tel: +90 212 723 69 00 Fax: +90 212 723 69 19
Web: www.artenova.com.tr, e-mail: info@artenova.com.tr

FAGOR ENDÜSTRİYEL SAN.
Tel: +90 262 751 10 31 Fax: +90 262 751 10 32
Web: www.fagor.com.tr, e-mail: fagor@fagor.com.tr

FATİH PLASTİK SAN.
Tel: +90 352 321 40 70
Web: www.fatihplastik.com, e-mail: info@fatihplastik.com

FETTAH ÇİNİ GIDA TEKSTİL TURİZM SAN. VE TİC. LTD. ŞTİ.
Tel: +90 274 266 22 02 Fax: +90 274 266 26 36
e-mail: fettahceramic@hotmail.com

FİL GRUP - FİLPA
Tel: +90 212 886 32 41 Fax: +90 212 886 32 64
Web: www.filgrup.com.tr, e-mail: info@filgrup.com.tr

FLORKİM
Tel: +90 216 466 82 72 pbx Fax: +90 216 365 23 05
Web: www.florkim.com, -mail: florkim@florkim.com

FORM KITCHEN APPLIANCES
Tel: +90 236 671 38 83 Fax: +90 212 671 38 84
Web: www.form-co.com, e-mail: form.co@form-co.com

FORM PLASTİK SAN. VE TİC. LTD. ŞTİ.
Tel: +90 236 214 01 13 Fax: +90 236 214 01 17
Web: www.formplastik.com.tr, e-mail: info@formplastik.com.tr

FRENOKS ENDÜSTRİYEL SOĞUTMA SANAYİ
Tel: +90 212 544 98 83 Fax: +90 212 493 42 11
Web: www.frenox.com, e-mail: info@frenox.com, burak@frenox.com

FRL FREELINE INDUSTRIAL CLEANING EQUIPMENTS
Tel: +90 212 674 75 75 Fax: +90 212 577 77 95
Web: www.freeline.com, e-mail: info@burcakplast.com.tr

GASTRODİZAYN INDUSTRIAL KITCHEN IND.
Tel: +90 212 297 11 00 Fax: +90 212 254 11 55
Web: www.gastrodizayn.com.tr, e-mail: gastrodizayn@gastrodizayn.com.tr

GD CRYSTAL
Tel: +90 212 613 74 47 Fax: +90 212 576 80 55
Web: www.gundogdukristal.com, e-mail: oktay@gundogdukristal.com

GLANGE CANDLES
Tel: +90 216 420 49 51 Fax: + 90 216 420 15 80
Web: www.glange.org, e-mail: info@glange.org

GLOBAL FOREIGN TRADE LTD. CO.
Tel: +90 258 211 83 57 Fax: +90 258 211 02 62
Web: www.globalcookware.com, e-mail: info@globalcookware.com

GLORE GLASSWARE - SAHRA CAM SAN.
Tel: +90 262 751 18 88 Fax: +90 262 751 18 69
Web: www.gloreglass.com, e-mail: info@gloreglass.com

GOLDEN FLORA
Tel: +90 216 328 64 27 Fax: +90 216 335 77 99
Web: www.goldenflora.com, e-mail: info@goldenflora .com

GOLDİNİ KRİSTAL
Tel: +90 216 320 51 41 Fax: +90 216 320 42 23
Web: www.goldini.com.tr, e-mail: info@goldini.com.tr

GONDOL PLASTIC INDUSTRY
Tel: +90 212 659 90 90 Fax: +90 212 659 87 77
Web: www.gondolplastic.com, e-mail: info@gondolplastic.com

GÖNEN METAL INDUSTRY
Tel: +90 212 552 25 08 Fax: +90 212 551 02 81
Web: www.biricik.com.tr, e-mail: biricik@biricik.com.tr

GÖRGEL METAL SAN. TİC. A.Ş.
Tel: +90 344 236 26 37 Fax: +90 344 236 30 90
Web: www.gorgelmetal.com.tr, e-mail: info@gorgelmetal.com.tr

GRAF IMPORT EXPORT AND TOURISM LTD. CO.
Tel: +90 212 482 02 25 Fax: +90 212 481 97 37
Web: www.graf.com.tr, e-mail: info@graf.com.tr

GRANİT DAYANIKLI TÜKETİM MALLARI
Tel: +90 232 853 91 00 Fax: +90 232 853 85 86
Web: www.granitltdsti.com.tr, e-mail: info@granitltdsti.com.tr

GUESTINHOUSE
Tel: +90 216 385 55 11 Fax: +90 216 385 55 13
Web: www.guestinhouse.com, e-mail: info@guestinhouse.com

GÜLİSTAN DEKAL ÇIKARTMA VE BASKI SAN.
Tel: +90 216 311 46 36 Fax: +90 216 311 36 50
Web: www.gulistandekal.com.tr, e-mail: gd@gulistandekal.com.tr

GÜNEŞ ENAMEL IND AND TRADE CO.
Tel: +90 212 512 95 69 Fax: + 90 212 520 02 60
Web: www.gunesmelamin.com, e-mail: ersan@gunesmelamin.com

GÜNEYSİ METAL MUTFAK EŞYALARI SAN.VE TİC.LTD.ŞTİ.
Tel: +90 344 236 00 15 Fax: +90 344 236 00 14
Web: www.guneysimetal.com.tr, e-mail: mehmet@guneysimetal.com.tr

GÜRÇELİK DAY. TÜK. MAM.
Tel: +90 232 853 92 00 Fax: +90 232 853 91 99
Web: www.gurcelik.com.tr, e-mail: gurcelik@gurcelik.com.tr

GÜREN METAL
Tel: +90 212 549 45 40 Fax: +90 212 549 45 39
Web: www.guren.com.tr, e-mail: info@guren.com.tr

GÜLBAK BAKALİT VE METAL SANAYİ TİCARET LTD. ŞTİ.
Tel: +90 344 236 46 26 Fax: +90 344 236 18 39
Web: www.gulbak.com.tr, e-mail: info@gulbak.com.tr

GÜNEŞ PLASTİK
Tel: +90 262 751 30 16 Fax: +90 262 751 25 00
Web: www.gunesplastik.com.tr, e-mail: info@gunesplastik.com.tr

GÜRAL PORCELAIN HERİŞ CERAMIC
Tel: +90 274 225 03 00 Fax: +90 274 225 03 16
Web: www.guralporselen.com.tr,
e-mail: export@guralporselen.com.tr

GÜRALLAR ARTCRAFT
Tel: +90 216 576 25 25 Fax: +90 216 576 25 00
Web: www.artcraft.com.tr
e-mail: artcraft@artcraft.com.tr

GÜR-PAK MELAMİN VE PLAST. SAN. VE TİC.LTD.ŞTİ
Tel: +90 212 486 23 01-02 Fax: +90 212 486 23 25
Web: www.euro-mel.com
e-mail: info@euro-mel.com, onur@euro-mel.com

GÜZELEV - MIACASA
Tel: +90 232 479 12 12 Fax: +90 232 479 92 48
Web: www.guzelev.com.tr, e-mail: info@guzelev.com.tr

HOUSEWARE
GIFTWARE
TABLEWARE
INDUSTRIAL
ELECTRICAL
PLASTICWARE
KITCHENWARE

63

turkish **kitchen** ware

GÜZELİŞ PORSELEN SAN. TİC. A.Ş. / Eternity
Tel: +90 216 598 35 35 Fax: +90 216 598 35 25
Web: www.guzelis.com.tr, e-mail: info@guzelis.com.tr

HAK PLASTİK AMBALAJ SAN.
Tel: +90 322 441 10 44 Fax: +90 322 441 02 44
Web: www.hakplastik.com.tr, e-mail: hakplastik@hakplastik.com.tr

HAKART DEKORATİF EŞYA VE METAL SAN. ve TİC. A.Ş.
Tel: +90 212 876 26 86 Fax: +90 212 876 26 88
Web: www.hakart.com.tr, e-mail: hakart@hakart.com.tr

HAMAM KONFEKSİYON PAZ.TEKS. SAN. TİC. LTD.ŞTİ.
Tel: +90 258 269 15 56 Fax: +90 258 269 15 59
Web: www.hamam.eu, e-mail: info@hamam.eu

HASCEVHER METAL SAN. / Hascevher, Hcm, Arian, Perfect
Tel: +90 344 257 95 70 Fax: +90 344 257 95 64
Web: www.hascevher.com.tr, e-mail: info@hascevher.com.tr

HAY FIRÇA SAN.
Tel: +90 232 264 60 17 Fax: + 90 232 264 76 10
Web: www.hayfirca.com, e-mail: info@hayfirca.com

HECHA CAST IRON COOKWARE FOR GOURMETS
Tel: +90 212 445 10 20 Fax: +90 212 445 79 79
Web: www.hecha.com.tr, e-mail: info@hecha.com.tr

HELENA SEDEFLİ MOBİLYA LTD. ŞTİ.
Tel: +90 326 285 62 08 Fax: +90 326 285 62 10
Web: www.helena.com.tr, e-mail: helena@helena.com.tr

HEREVIN SOLMAZER KITCHENWARE INDUSTRY LTD / Herevin, Mayamos
Tel: +90 212 659 00 19 Fax: +90 212 659 40 46
Web: www.solmazer.com, e-mail: info@solmazer.com
export@solmazer.com

Hİ-PAŞ PLASTİK EŞYA TİC.VE SAN.LTD.ŞTİ.
Tel: +90 212 659 03 86 Fax: +90 212 659 03 80
Web: www.evelin.com.tr, www.hipas.com.tr
e-mail: info@evelin.com.tr; info@hipas.com.tr

HİREF TASARIM ORG. VE DIŞ TİC.
Tel: +90 212 283 15 77 Fax: +90 212 283 15 78
Web: www.hiref.com.tr, e-mail: info@hirefstore.com.tr

HİSAR CUTLERY AND COOKWARE PRODUCT
Tel: +90 212 596 10 03 Fax: +90 212 596 10 35
Web: www.hisar.com.tr, e-mail: export@hisar.com.tr

HOMATEX TURİZM VE OTEL MALZ.
Tel: +90 212 320 32 55 Fax: +90 212 320 32 50
Web: www.homatex.com.tr, e-mail: homatex@homatex.com.tr

HOTEC TOURISM IND IMPORT EXPORT
Tel: +90 212 320 30 70 Fax: +90 212 221 33 74
Web: www.hotecturkey.com, e-mail: esene@hotecturkey.com

HÜRSULTAN CO.
Tel: +90 212 798 25 60 Fax: +90 212 798 25 69
Web: www.hursultan.com.tr, e-mail: info@hursultan.com.tr

ICF KITCHEN APPLIANCES
Tel: +90 216 575 51 54 Fax: +90 216 572 44 27
Web: www.icfappliances.com, e-mail: cenk@icfappliances.com

ILIO
Tel: +90 212 245 25 63 Fax: +90 212 244 89 43
Web: www.demirden.com, e-mail: info@demirden.com

INDESIT COMPANY
Tel: +90 212 355 53 00 Fax: +90 212 216 13 73
Web: www.hotpoint.com.tr

IRAK PLASTİK SANAYİ
Tel: +90 212 659 54 12 Fax: + 90 212 659 51 08
Web: www.irakplast.com, e-mail: expo@irakplast.com,
pazarlama@irakplast.com, sibel@irakplast.com

ISITAŞ BEYAZ EŞYA SAN. VE TİC. A.Ş.
Tel: +90 222 236 16 63 - 64 Fax: +90 222 236 16 65
Web: www.sunfire.com.tr, e-mail: export@sunfire.com.tr

IŞILAY MUTFAK EŞYALARI BAKALİT METAL TEKS.TAŞ.İNŞ.GIDA SAN.TİC.LTD.STİ.
Tel: +90 344 236 09 64 Fax: +90 344 236 09 75
e-mail: info@isilaymetal.com

İKRA METAL STANLIESS STEEL INDUSTRY
Tel: +90 344 236 40 00 Fax: +90 344 236 40 40
Web: www.ikragroup.com, e-mail: ikratrade@ikragroup.com

İLYASOĞLU EVIL EYES
Tel: +90 212 513 34 49 Fax: +90 212 310 24 95
Web: www.ilyasoglu.com, e-mail: contact@ilyasoglu.com

İNCİ MADENİ EŞYA
Tel: +90 212 597 60 34 Fax: +90 212 597 52 13
Web: www.incicelik.com.tr, e-mail: incicelik@incicelik.com.tr

İNOKSAN A.Ş. / İnoksdesign, Klinoks
Tel: +90 224 294 74 74 Fax: +90 224 243 61 23
Web: www.inoksan.com.tr, e-mail: inoksan@inoksan.com.tr

İPEK ZÜC. IMPORT & EXPORT CO. LTD.
Tel: +90 212 659 24 28 Fax: +90 212 659 55 30
Web: www.ipekltd.com, e-mail: export@carmelia.com.tr

İTİMAT MAKİNA SANAYİ
Tel: +90 352 321 26 26 Fax: +90 352 321 18 03
Web: www.itimat.com.tr, e-mail: itimat@itimat.com.tr

İZMAK INDUSTRIAL KITCHEN EQUIPMENTS MANUFACTURER
Tel: +90 232 281 44 64 Fax: +90 232 281 51 25
Web: www.izmak.com.tr, e-mail: izmak@izmak.com.tr

JUMBO MADENİ MUTFAK EŞYA SAN.
Tel: +90 212 565 90 70 Fax: +90 212 565 60 47
Web: www.jumbo.com.tr, e-mail: info@jumbo.com.tr

KABOĞLU PLASTIC PACKAGING IND. TRADE
Tel: +90 216 304 04 24 Fax: +90 216 304 02 29
Web: www.kabogluplastik.com, faruk@kabogluplastik.com

KALIPSAN KALIP PLASTİK VE AMBALAJ SAN.
Tel: +90 212 422 92 43 Fax: +90 212 422 68 85
Web: www.kalipsanplastik.com.tr
e-mail: info@kalipsanplastik.com.tr

KALİTE INDUSTRIAL KITCHEN APPLIANCES IND.
Tel: +90 212 671 99 34 Fax: + 90 212 671 99 44
Web: www.kalitegaz.com.tr, e-mail: info@kalitegaz.com.tr

KAR MAKİNA PARÇALARI SAN. / Omg Innova
Tel: +90 262 751 03 90 Fax: +90 262 751 03 94
Web: www.omginnova.com e-mail: mustafa@omginnova.com

KAR TEKNİK SOĞUTMA ENDÜSTRİYEL MUTFAK SAN.
Tel: +90 242 258 18 50 Fax: +90 242 258 18 55
Web: www.karteknik.com, karteknik@karteknik.com

KARACA ZÜCCACİYE TİC. SAN. A.Ş.
Tel: +90 212 412 44 00 Fax: +90 212 422 48 59
Web: www.krc.com.tr, e-mail: krc@krc.com.tr

KARAKAYA PLASTIC LTD. ŞTİ.
Tel: +90 212 567 23 19 Fax: +90 212 577 06 94
Web: www.karakayaplastik.com, e-mail: karakaya@karakayaplastik.com

KARAT TAKI VE MÜCEVHERAT SAN. TİC. A.Ş.
Tel: +90 232 462 06 06 Fax: +90 232 462 05 05
Web: www.karatgold.com.tr, e-mail: info@karatgold.com.tr

KARDESAN BAKERY AND PASTRY EQUIPMENTS
Tel: +90 216 471 84 61 Fax: +90 216 471 84 62
Web: www.kardesan.com, e-mail: info@kardesan.com

KARTAL INDUSTRIAL KITCHEN APPLIANCES
Tel: +90 212 428 09 04 Fax: +90 212 428 09 07
Web: www.kartalmutfak.com,e-mail: info@kartalmutfak.com

KASTAMONU PLASTİK PACKAGING PRODUCTS
Tel: +90 212 509 32 99 Fax: +90 212 676 39 06
Web: www.kastamonuplastik.com, e-mail: info@kastamonuplastik.com

KAVSAN
Tel: +90 212 552 01 39 Fax: +90 212 522 40 71
Web: www.kavsan.com, e-mail: kavsan@kavsan.com

KAYALAR ENDÜSTRİYEL MUTFAK SANAYİ /
Folnox, Electromax, Mastro
Tel: +90 212 612 26 11 Fax: +90 212 493 10 16
Web: www.kayalarmutfak.com
e-mail: info@kayalarmutfak.com

KAYALAR STEEL CO.
Tel: +90 212 859 00 02 Fax: +90 212 859 00 14
Web: www.kayalar.com.tr, e-mail: kayalar@kayalar.com.tr

KAYALAR MUTFAK-OTEL-RESTAURANT EKİPMANLARI
Tel: +90 232 479 79 90 Fax: + 90 232 479 79 94
Web: www.kayalar.gen.tr
e-mail: osman@kayalar.gen.tr

KERAMİKA SERAMİK
Tel: +90 274 266 20 02 Fax: +90 274 266 24 55
Web: www.keramika.com.tr, e-mail: fyuce@unsamadencilik.com.tr

KILIÇLAR ÇATAL KAŞIK MADENİ MUTFAK EŞYALARI
Tel: +90 216 592 82 00 Fax: +90 216 592 24 55
Web: www.kiliclar.net, e-mail: kiliclar@superonline.com

KING PAZARLAMA VE DIŞ TİC. A.Ş.
Tel: +90 212 565 15 95 Fax: +90 212 565 16 07
Web: www.king.com.tr, e-mail: pazarlama@king.com.tr

KIRTEKSMETAL TEKSTİL SAN. VE TİC. LTD.ŞTİ.
Tel: +90 344 257 91 43 Fax: +90 344 257 91 46
Web: www.kirteksmetal.com, e-mail: info@kirteksmetal.com

KIZIKOĞLU INDUSTRIAL COOLING INDUSTRY
Tel: +90 274 224 93 92 Fax: +90 274 224 93 90
Web: www.sogutmaci.com, e-mail: export@sogutmaci.com

KLASS FOREIGN TRADE LTD. CO.
Tel: +90 352 321 13 79 Fax: +90 352 321 18 43
Web: www.klass.com.tr, e-mail: info@klass.com.tr
export.class@gmail.com

KLEO MINIBAR & ROOM SERVICE EQUIPMENTS
Tel: +90 242 321 46 76 Fax: +90 242 321 47 17
Web: www.minibar.com.tr, e-mail: info@minibar.com.tr

KONYA SARAYLI MADENİ EŞYA / Saraylı
Tel: +90 332 239 08 78 Fax: +90 332 239 02 36
Web: www.smsarayli.com.tr, e-mail: info@smsarayli.com.tr

KORKMAZ STAINLESS STEEL COOKWARE & ELECTRICAL
Tel: +90 216 444 01 47 Fax: +90 216 540 09 34
Web: www.korkmaz.com.tr, e-mail: info@korkmaz.com.tr

KRISTAL INDUSTRIAL
Tel: +90 242 258 03 22 Fax: +90 242 258 00 68
Web: www.kristalendustriyel.com
mail: info@kristalendustriyel.com, u.acar@ kristalendustriyel.com

KROMÇELİK STAINLESS STEEL SINKS
Tel: +90 212 771 53 53 Fax: +90 212 771 53 63
Web: www.kromcelik.com.tr, e-mail: info@kromcelik.com.tr

KROMEVYE SAN. TİC. LTD. ŞTİ.
Tel: +90 212 886 55 88 (pbx) Fax: +90 212 886 57 14
Web: www.kromevye.com.tr, e-mail: info@kromevye.com.tr

HOUSEWARE • GIFTWARE • TABLEWARE • INDUSTRIAL • ELECTRICAL • PLASTICWARE • KITCHENWARE •

KROMLÜKS MUTFAK CİHAZLARI
Tel: +90 312 231 84 50 Fax: +90 312 231 45 92
Web: www.kromluks.com, e-mail: kromluks@kromluks.com

KÜÇÜK ESNAF TURİSTİK EŞYA İMALATI
Tel: +90 212 511 23 62 Fax: +90 212 511 23 62
Web: www.artmosaiclamp.com, e-mail: info@artmosaiclamp.com

KÜLSAN ENAMEL PLASTIC
Tel: +90 212 477 56 66 Fax: + 90 212 618 19 70
Web: www.kulsan.com.tr, e-mail: kulsan@kulsan.com.tr

KÜTAHYA PORSELEN SAN. A.Ş.
Tel: +90 274 225 01 50 Fax: +90 274 225 12 08
Web: www.kutahyaporselen.com.tr
e-mail: nmercan@kutahyaporselen.com

LAVA METAL DÖKÜM SAN. TİC. A.Ş.
Tel: +90 216 312 26 53 Fax: +90 216 312 09 09
Web: www.lavametal.com.tr
e-mail: satis@lavametal.com.tr

LEYDİ NON-STICK COOKWARE
Tel: +90 212 659 54 67
Web: www.leydimutfak.com, e-mail: leydi@leydimutfak.com

LSB DIŞ TİC. VE DAN. LTD. ŞTİ.
Tel: +90 216 413 82 53 Fax: +90 216 425 46 59
Web: www.lsbgroup.com
e-mail: info@lsbgroup.com, mesutbudak@lsbgroup.com

LUX PLASTIC / Avantage, Bosfor, Seher, Avantaj Ev
Tel: +90 212 659 11 26 Fax: +90 212 659 25 46
Web: www.luxplastic.com, e-mail: info@luxplastic.com

LUYANO ZÜCCACİYE TEKSTİL SAN. VE TİC. LTD. ŞTİ.
Tel: +90 212 292 31 63 Fax: +90 212 292 31 49
Web: www.luyano.com.tr, e-mail: info@luyano.com.tr

MAIN STEEL TRADE LTD. CO.
Tel: +90 212 875 42 00 Fax: +90 212 875 42 09
Web: www.maintuna.com, e-mail: info@maintuna.com

MAKPA A.Ş.
Tel: +90 212 256 83 50 Fax: +90 212 250 40 53
Web: www.makpa.com, e-mail: istmakpa@makpa.com

MAKSAN MUTFAK SANAYİ VE TİC. LTD. ŞTİ.
Tel: +90 232 254 29 17 Fax: +90 232 281 33 11
Web: www.maksanmutfak.com, e-mail: info@maksanmutfak.com

MASKOT MUTFAK EŞYALARI
Tel: +90 212 435 55 85 Fax: +90 212 435 42 58
Web: www.maskotmutfak.com, e-mail: info@maskotmutfak.com

MASTER MUTFAK CİHAZLARI
Tel: +90 212 485 85 30 Fax: + 90 212 485 85 34
Web: www.mastermutfak.com, Web: mastermutfak@mastermutfak.com

MAYAPAZ
Tel: +90 212 468 18 92 Fax: +90 212 476 21 58
Web: www.mayapaz.com.tr, e-mail: info@mayapaz.com.tr

MAYSA MADENİ EŞYA SANAYİ VE TİCARET LTD. ŞTİ.
Tel: +90 352 321 12 83 Fax: +90 352 321 12 00
Web: www.maysa.com.tr, e-mail: maysa@maysa.com.tr

MEGA MADENİ EV GEREÇLERİ
Tel: +90 258 251 69 90 Fax: +90 258 251 66 10
Web: www.boztepe.com, e-mail: info@boztepe.com

MEHTAP COOKWARE / Mehtap, Sms
Tel: +90 216 419 67 62 Fax: +90 216 419 67 64
Web: www.mehtap.com.tr, e-mail: info@mehtap.com.tr

MELTEM CUTLERY INC.
Tel: +90 212 642 32 86 Fax: +90 212 642 32 88
Web: www.meltemcatal.com.tr, e-mail: info@meltemcatal.com.tr

MELTEM-METIN EMAYE SAC SANAYİ VE TİCARET
Tel: +90 216 394 35 86 Fax: +90 216 394 35 92
Web: www.meltemgas.com, e-mail: sales@meltemgas.com

MERİH METAL INDUSTRY
Tel: +90 212 493 21 56 Fax: +90 212 567 75 80
Web: www.merihmetal.com.tr, e-mail: info@merihmetal.com.tr

MERT GIFT SHOP
Tel: +90 212 526 04 81 Fax: +90 212 526 04 81
Web: www.mertgift.com, e-mail: info@mertgift.com

MESSI EV VE MUTFAK EŞYALARI SAN.
Tel: +90 212 485 51 97 Fax: +90 212 485 51 98
Web: www.ardivasilver.com.tr
e-mail: info@ardivasilver.com

MEŞALE ÇAY OCAĞI KAZANLAR GIDA VE TEKSTİL SAN.
Tel: +90 212 418 00 00 Fax: +90 212 581 58 82
Web: www.mesale.com, e-mail: info@mesale.com

METE PLASTİK SANAYİ TİC.
Tel: +90 212 875 43 33 Fax: +90 212 875 33 03
Web: www.mete.com.tr, e-mail: meteplast@mete.com.tr

MİLENYUM METAL DIŞ TİC. VE SAN. LTD. ŞTİ
Tel: +90 352 311 44 54 Fax: +90 352 311 34 17
Web: www.palm.com.tr, e-mail: export@palm.com.tr

MİMAR SİNAN KITCHENWARE IND.
Tel: +90 212 422 90 94 Fax: +90 212 422 41 84
Web: www.mimarsinancelik.com,
e-mail: emine@mimarsinancelik.com

MİZAN EV GEREÇLERİ PLASTİK İNŞAAT LTD.ŞTİ.
Tel: +90 212 659 27 45 Fax: +90 212 659 27 03
Web: www.mizanplastic.com
e-mail: info@mizanplastic.com

MN-SKALA DEKORASYON
Tel: +90 312 349 02 95 Fax: +90 312 349 11 30
Web: www.deykimskala.com, e-mail: info@deykimskala.com

MONNA GLASS
Tel: +90 212 886 25 93 Fax: +90 212 886 25 97
Web: www.monnaglass.com, e-mail: info@monnaglass.com

MUTAŞ GROUP
Tel: +90 312 363 99 33 Fax: +90 312 363 94 92
Web: www.vitalmutfak.com, e-mail: info@vitalmutfak.com

MUTLU METAL SAN. VE TİC. A.Ş.
Tel: +90 232 853 74 44 Fax: +90 232 853 74 14
Web: www.mutlumetal.com.tr, e-mail: info@mutlumetal.com

MYTH ARTS
Tel: +90 212 249 09 53 Fax: +90 212 249 09 54
Web: www.myth.com.tr, e-mail: info@myth.com.tr

NARİN MADENİ EŞYA SAN. / Narin
Tel: +90 212 630 84 34 Fax: +90 212 550 38 15
Web: www.narinmetal.com, e-mail: ahunarin@narinmetal.com
info@narinmetal.com

NATSAN CO. LTD.
Tel: +90 212 605 02 65 Fax: +90 212 605 02 68
Web: www.natsan.com.tr, e-mail: info@natsan.com.tr

NATUREL DTM. MOB. SAN.
Tel: +90 352 322 20 25 Fax: +90 352 322 20 30
Web: www. naturelocak.com
e-mail: mali@naturelocak.com
mustafayayar@naturelocak.com

NDUSTRIO
Tel: +90 216 59302 42 Fax: +90 216 593 02 43
Web: www.ndustrio.com, e-mail: info@ndustrio.com

NECATİ ATLI-ATLI ÇELİK METAL SANAYİ
Tel: +90 344 236 08 51 Fax: +90 344 236 39 15
Web: www.atlicelik.com, e-mail: info@atlicelik.com

NEHİR MADENİ MUTFAK EŞYA SAN.
Tel: +90 212 656 65 50 Fax: +90 212 651 75 71
Web: www.nehir.com, e-mail: nehir@nehir.com.tr

NEPTÜN DIŞ TİC.A.Ş
Tel: +90 216 343 34 38 Fax: +90 216 334 93 79
Web: www.neptunev.com
e-mail: merve@neptunev.com - doruk@neptunev.com

NETLON MUTFAK ARAÇLARI / Netlon, Netlife
Tel: +90 212 270 44 91 Fax: +90 212 280 50 95
Web: www.netlon.com.tr, e-mail: bernay@netcelik.com.tr

NOUVAL GROUP MUTFAK EŞYALARI
Tel: +90 212 445 40 00 Fax: + 90 212 445 30 20
Web: www.nouvalgroup.com, e-mail: nouval@nouval.com.tr

OBJE PLASTİK TASARIM REKLAM ÜRÜNLERİ SAN.VE TİC.
Tel: +90 212 674 39 24 Fax: +90 212 567 52 34
Web: www.objeplastik.com
e-mail: info@objeplastik.com; sami@objeplastik.com

OĞUZHAN PLASTİK VE KALIP SAN.
Tel: +90 212 485 99 18 Fax: +90 212 485 99 52
Web: www.vialli.com.tr, e-mail: info@vialli.com.tr

OKYANUS MUTFAK EŞYALARI SAN. VE DIŞ TİC. LTD. ŞTİ.
Tel: +90 212 659 51 54 Fax: +90 212 659 56 10
Web: www.okyanushome.com, e-mail: info@okyanushome.com

OMS KITCHENWARE LTD. / Oms, Didem, Oms Kitchen Star, Oms Kinox, Oms Solingen
Tel: +90 212 689 05 23 Fax: +90 212 689 05 97
Web: www.omscollection.com
e-mail: info@omscolection.com, aysun@omscolection.com

ONUR BAKALİT VE METAL SAN. TİC. A.Ş
Tel: +90 212 344 236 28 00 Fax: +90 212 344 236 28 05
Web: www.onurbakalit.com.tr, e-mail: veli@onurbakalit.com.tr

ONUR MADENİ EŞYA SAN. VE TİC. LTD. ŞTİ
Tel: +90 212 537 99 08 Fax: +90 212 617 91 63
e-mail: seliminci@onursteel.com

ORGAZ GAZ ALET. SAN. VE TİC. LTD. ŞTİ.
Tel: +90 216 593 93 93 Fax: +90 216 593 93 94
Web: www.orgaz.com.tr, e-mail: info@orgaz.com.tr

ORMEL OTEL RESTAURANT MUTFAK EKİPMANLARI SAN.
Tel: +90 212 321 01 02 Fax: +90 212 321 01 03
Web: www.ormel.com.tr, e-mail: ormel@ormel.com.tr

OS-KAR METAL SAN. TİC. LTD. ŞTİ.
Tel: +90 212 558 76 46 Fax: +90 212 558 76 56
Web: www.oscarsink.com, e-mail: oskarmetal@hotmail.com

OTTOMAN DIŞ TİC. VE MUTFAK GEREÇLERİ
Tel: +90 212 670 41 75 Fax: +90 212 670 48 84
Web: www.ottomanmutfak.com.tr, e-mail: info@ottomanmutfak.com

OTS METAL SAN. TİC. LTD.ŞTİ.
Tel: +90 212 613 80 30 Fax: +90 212 613 80 37
Web: www.otsmetal.com, e-mail: info@otsmetal.com

ÖDÜL MADENİ EŞYA SAN. TİC. VE LTD. ŞTİ.
Tel: +90 352 321 38 53 Fax: +90 352 321 38 52
Web: www.odul.com.tr, e-mail: yahsi@odul.com.tr

ÖNCÜ MUTFAK EŞYALARI SAN.TİC.LTD.ŞTİ.
Tel: +90 344 236 33 23 Fax: +90 344 236 03 49
Web: www.oncu.com.tr, e-mail: info@oncu.com.tr

ÖZAY TRAY CO.
Tel: +90 262 751 29 40 Fax: +90 262 751 18 79
Web: www.ozaytray.com.tr, e-mail: hdiktas@ozaytray.com

HOUSEWARE
GIFTWARE
TABLEWARE
INDUSTRIAL
ELECTRICAL
PLASTICWARE
KITCHENWARE

67

ÖZBİR METAL PASL. ÇELİK SAN. TİC. LTD. ŞTİ.
Tel: +90 212 615 54 13 Fax: +90 212 615 07 09
Web: www.ozbirmetal.com, e-mail: info@ozbirmetal.com

ÖZDEMİR KARDEŞLER KITCHEN EQUIPMENTS
Tel: +90 212 615 64 30 Fax: +90 212 615 07 09
Web: www.ozdemirkardesler.com
Contact: Turgut Özdemir, e-mail: info@ozdemirkardes.com.tr

ÖZGÜL MUTFAK EŞYALARI SAN.VE TİC.LTD.ŞTİ.
Tel: +90 344 236 64 00 Fax: +90 344 236 26 27
Web: www.ozgulmelamin.com., e-mail: info@ozgulmelamin.com.

ÖZ-ER PLASTİK SAN. VE TİC. LTD. ŞTİ.
Tel: +90 212 886 94 94 Fax: +90 212 886 94 96
Web: www.ozerplastik.com, e-mail: info@ozerplastik.com

ÖZMET A.Ş.
Tel: +90 212 886 88 00 Fax: +90 212 886 68 17
Web: www.oztiryakiler.com.tr, e-mail: ozmet@oztiryakiler.com.tr

ÖZMETAL STAINLESS STEEL IND. AND TRADE LTD. CO.
Tel: +90 212 547 44 71 (pbx) Fax: +90 212 558 76 46
Web: www.ozmetal.com.tr, e-mail: ozmetal@ozmetal.com.tr

ÖZMEN EMAYE SAN.
Tel: +90 352 321 35 51 Fax: +90 352 321 35 54
Web: www.ozmengroup.com.tr
e-mail: ozmen@ozmengroup.com

ÖZTİRYAKİLER METAL GOODS INDUSTRY/
equipmentsi Oven, Fryer, Gril, Cooker
Tel: 212 886 78 00 Fax: +90 212 886 78 09
Web: www.oztiryakiler.com.tr, e-mail: export@oztiryakiler.com.tr,
doztiryaki@oztiryakiler.com.tr

ÖZTİRYAKİLER PORSELEN A.Ş.
Tel: +90 212 886 88 00 Fax: +90 212 886 78 09
Web:www.oztiryakiler.com.tr, e-mail: oztiryakiler@oztiryakiler.com.tr

PAKSAN İÇ VE DIŞ TİC.
Tel: +90 212 519 06 01 / 528 00 53 Fax: +90 212 512 24 46
Web: www.paksan.info, e-mail: paksan@paksan.info

PAN MUTFAK EŞYALARI SAN.TİC.LTD.ŞTİ
Tel: +90 262 353 44 34 Fax: +90 262 353 45 69
Web: www.soli.com.tr, e-mail: rustem.zaloglu@soli.com.tr
info@soli.com.tr

PDS SAĞLIK VE GIDA EKİPMANLARI / Soft Bowl, Silicopan,Babysoft
Tel: +90 212 613 15 66 Fax: +90 212 612 71 95
Web: www.pds.com.tr, e-mail: info@pds.com.tr

PASDEKOR SÜSLEME VE DEKORASYON MALZ. SAN.
Tel: +90 212 235 11 11 Fax: +90 212 361 19 99
Web: www.pasdekor.com.tr,
e-mail:info@pasdekor.com.tr

PAŞABAHÇE / Paşabahçe, F&d, Denizli, Borcam
Tel: +90 212 350 50 50 Fax: +90 212 350 50 47
Web: www.pasabahce.com.tr,
e-mail: osagiroglu@sisecam.com
sucaliskan@sisecam.com

PİRGE - YEŞİLYAYLA CUTLERY TOOLS CO.
Tel: +90 224 216 01 02 Fax: +90 224 215 28 00
Web: www.pirge.com, e-mail: ömer@pirge.com
info@pirge.com

PLASBAK PLASTİK ENJEKSİYON VE KALIP SAN.TİC.LTD.ŞTİ.
Tel: +90 212 875 03 46 fax: +90 212 875 18 11
Web:www.plasbak.com, e-mail:info@plasbak.com

PORLAND PORSELEN SANAYİ
Tel: +90 262 648 59 00 Fax: +90 262 754 15 61
Web: www.porland.com.tr, e-mail: gebze@porland.com.tr

RENGA - MERCANLAR MUTFAK EŞYALARI SANAYİ / Renga, Tassar
Tel: +90 212 875 44 55 Fax: +90 212 876 67 42
Web: www.mercanlarkitchen.com, e-mail: export@ mercanlarkitchen.com

RİTİM HEDİYELİK VE AKSESUAR
Tel: +90 212 279 25 83 Fax: +90 212 279 34 49
Web: www.ritim.com.tr, e-mail: ritim@ritim.com.tr

ROSITELL PLASTIC INDUSTRY
Tel: +90 236 214 01 03 Fax: +90 236 214 00 52
Web: www.rositell.com, e-mail: info@rositell.com

SAFLON METAL SANAYİ
Tel: +90 344 623 10 29 Fax: +90 344 623 10 29
Web: www.saflon.com, e-mail: info@saflon.com

SAM METAL TOKA
Tel: +90 212 549 87 22 Fax: +90 212 549 87 30
Web: www.sammetal.com, e-mail: hüseyin@sammetal.com.tr

SANİFOAM SÜNGER SAN. VE TİC. A.Ş.
Tel: +90 212 438 53 00 Fax: +90 212 438 53 53
Web: www.sanifoam.com.tr
e-mail: uyilmaz@sanifoam.com.tr, info@sanifoam.com.tr

SAREX ELEKTRİKLİ EV ALETLERİ
Tel: +90 212 471 11 11 Fax: +90 212 471 12 12
Web: www.sarex.gen.tr, e-mail: info@sarex.net

SAVAŞAN EMAYE VE SOBA SAN. / Grandeur
Tel: +90 332 334 05 50 Fax: +90 332 335 05 60
Web: www.savasan.com, e-mail: savasan@savasan.com

SELECT EV AKSESUARLARI SAN.VE TİC.LTD.ŞTİ.
Tel: +90 212 243 00 00 fax: +90 212 243 00 02
Web:www.select.com.tr, e-mail: seckinsaglam@select.com.tr

SEM PLASTİK SAN/ Sem, Sem E-Lite Plus
Tel: +90 212 736 07 37 Fax: +90 212 736 07 27
Web: www.semplastik.com.tr, e-mail: info@semplastik.com.tr

SENUR
Tel: +90 212 422 19 10 Fax: +90 212 422 09 29
Web: www.senur.com.tr
e-mail: serhan@senur.com.tr, info @senur.com.tr

SERKAN METAL SAN.
Tel: +90 212 689 40 44 Fax: +90 212 689 40 48
Web: www.camino.com.tr
e-mail: info@camino.com.tr

SEVAL ALUMİNYUM BAKALİT ÇELİK PAZARLAMA VE SAN.TİC.LTD.ŞTİ.
Tel: +90 344 236 22 66 Fax: +90 344 236 05 39
Web: www.sevalcelik.com.tr, e-mail: info@sevalcelik.com.tr

SEYEKS DIŞ TİC.
Tel: +90 216 345 50 96 Fax: +90 216 337 17 46
Web: www.seyeks.com, e-mail: seyeks@seyeks.com

SGS MUTFAK EKİPMANLARI
Tel: +90 232 257 52 23 Fax: +90 232 257 53 03
Web: www.sgsoven.com, e-mail: info@sgsoven.com

SİDE ÇELİK
Tel: +90 344 236 44 55 Fax: +90 344 236 02 18
Web: www.sidecelik.com.tr, e-mail: info@sidecelik.com.tr

SILVER İÇ VE DIŞ TİC.A.Ş.
Tel: +90 352 241 01 90 Fax: +90 352 241 01 94
Web: www.silver.com.tr, e-mail: foreingtrade@silver.com.tr

SILVERLINE BUILT APPLIENCES
Tel: +90 212 484 48 00 Fax: +90 212 481 40 08
Web: www.silverlineappliances.com
e-mail: info@silverlineappliances.com

SINBO HOUSEHOLD APPLIENCES
Tel: +90 212 422 94 94
Web: www.sinbo.com.tr, e-mail: info@sinbo.com.tr

SNT TOPRAK ÜRÜNLERİ
Tel: +90 228 381 47 60 Fax: +90 228 381 43 26
Web: www.sntstoneware.com, e-mail: info@sntstoneware.com.tr

STAR MUTFAK VE MOBİLYA
Tel: +90 212 855 65 65 Fax: +90 212 855 68 70
Web: www.starax.com.tr, e-mail: staraksesuar.com.tr

STAR TEMİZLİK MAKİNALARI
Tel: +90 216 572 74 04 Fax: +90 216 572 92 25
Web: www.starmakina.com.tr, e-mail: star@starmakina.com.tr

SUN METAL
Tel: +90 212 475 99 66 Fax: +90 212 475 08 82
Web: www.sunmetal.net, e-mail: info@sunmetal.net

SUN PLASTIC HOUSEWARE / suncook, Sunday, Sunbath, Sunfix
Tel: +90 212 659 05 05 Fax: +90 212 659 59 60
Web: www.sunplastik.com.tr
e-mail: info@sunplastik.com.tr

ŞENİNOKS INDUSTRIAL
Tel: +90 212 221 15 95 Fax: +90 212 221 54 79
Web: www.seninoks.com, e-mail: info@seninoks.com

ŞENSOY MADENİ EŞYA VE KALIP SAN. TİC. LTD. ŞTİ.
Tel: +90 212 549 39 25 Fax: +90 212 549 15 16
Web: www.seden.com.tr,
e-mail: cansu@seden.com.tr, info@seden.com.tr

ŞENYAYLA PLS. SAN. VE TİC. A.Ş.
Tel: +90 212 514 16 93 Fax: +90 212 513 90 01
Web: www.senyayla.com, e-mail: senyayla@senyayla.com

ŞİRİN PLASTİK
Tel: +90 212 501 21 47 Fax: +90 212 577 54 96
Web: www.sirinplastik.com.tr, e-mail: info@sirinplastik.com.tr

TAÇ MUTFAK EŞYALARI/ Taç, Aksu, Vallena, Emprassa
Tel: +90 212 691 06 21 Fax: + 90 212 691 06 32
Web: www.tacmutfak.com, e-mail: info@tacmutfak.com

TAMLAS OTO LAS. MLZ. SAN. VE TİC. LTD. ŞTİ.
Tel: +90 352 694 51 76 Fax: +90 352 694 51 02
Web: www.tamlas.com.tr, e-mail: info@tamlas.com

TANTİTONİ (İnter Mutfak Eşyaları Tic. A.Ş.)
Tel: +90 212 293 02 93 Fax: +90 212 292 49 88
Web: www.tantitoni.com.tr, e-mail: info@intermutfak.com.tr

TAŞHAN MUTFAK
Tel: +90 212 683 00 69 Fax: +90 212 683 00 67
Web: www.tashanmutfak.com.tr, e-mail: info@tashanmutfak.com.tr

TEK-ART HEDİYELİK EŞYA
Tel: +90 216 433 33 00 Fax: +90 216 433 33 10
Web: www.tek-art.com.tr, e-mail: info@tek-art.com.tr

TEKA TEKNİK MUTFAK ALETLERİ
Tel: +90 212 886 95 00 34 Fax: +90 212 274 56 86
Web: www.teka.com, e-mail: cenk.cınar@teka.com.tr

TEKNO-TEL
Tel: +90 212 659 16 50 Fax: +90 212 659 17 53
Web: www.tekno-tel.com, e-mail: info@tekno-tel.com.tr

TEKNOGRAND SOĞUTMA SAN.
Tel: +90 212 299 68 64 Fax: +90 212 277 13 24
Web: www.teknogrand.com, e-mail: info@teknogrand.com

TEKPLAS PLASTİK DAY. TÜK. MAL.
İTH.İHR.SAN.VE TİC.LTD.ŞTİ.
Tel: +90 352 321 30 37 Fax: +90 352 321 30 38
Web: www.tekplas.com, e-mail: galaxy@tekplas.com

TEKSAN HOME APPLIANCES
Tel: +90 212 685 07 43 Fax: +90 212 685 29 50
Web: www.teksanevgerecleri.com
e-mail: teksan@teksanevgerecleri.com

TERMO GLASS IND.
Tel: +90 212 886 25 83 Fax: +90 212 886 25 88
Web: www.termocam.com, e-mail: export@termocam.com

TİTİZ PLASTİK DIŞ TİCARET
Tel: +90 212 798 24 90 Fax: +90 212 798 24 99
Web: www.titizplastik.com, e-mail: export@titizplastik.com

TOLKAR INDUSTRIAL CUANDRY & GARMENT / Tolkar, Smartex
Tel: +90 232 376 85 00 Fax: +90 232 376 76 58
Web: www.tolkar.com.tr
e-mail: info@tolkar.com.tr

TRINOKS EVYE METAL SAN. TİC. LTD. ŞTİ.
Tel: +90 212 486 39 12 Fax: +90 212 486 39 14
Web: www.trinoxevye.com
e-mail: y.asnas@trinoxevye.com

● HOUSEWARE ● GIFTWARE ● TABLEWARE ● INDUSTRIAL ● ELECTRICAL ● PLASTICWARE ● KITCHENWARE

TURAN PLASTİK SAN. NAK. VE TİC. LTD. ŞTİ.
Tel: +90 462 711 43 61 Fax: +90 462 71143 62
Web: www.turanplastic.com.tr
e-mail: info@turanplastic.com

TUTKU METAL
Tel: +90 344 251 33 43 Fax: +90 344 251 33 29
Web: www.tutkumetal.com.tr, e-mail: info@tutkumetal.com

TÜRMAK MAKİNE
Tel: +90 212 281 51 04 Fax: +90 212 281 51 07
Web: www.turmak.com, e-mail: turmak@turmak.com.

UFUK METAL SAN.VE TİC. LTD.ŞTİ.
Tel: +90 344 236 01 30 Fax: +90 344 236 01 33
Web:www.ufukartglass.com, e-mail: uygar@ufukartglass.com
info@ufukartglass.com

UKINOX KITCHEN SYSTEMS INC.
Tel: +90 212 886 91 95 Fax: +90 212 886 91 95
Web: www.ukinox.com
e-mail: info@ukinox.com, export@ukinox.com,

ULUDAĞ MUTFAK SANAYİ
Tel: +90 224 256 62 32 Fax: +90 224 272 15 13
Web: www.uludagmutfak.com.tr
e-mail: info@uludagmutfak.com.tr

**ULUTAŞ METAL MUTFAK EŞYALARI
İNŞAAT SAN.VE TİC. A.Ş.**
Tel: +90 344 251 27 46 Fax: +90 344 251 27 45
e-mail: ulutascelik@hotmail.com

UTG DIŞ TİC
Tel: +90 232 441 41 90 Fax: +90 232 441 01 81
Web: www.ultratech.com.tr, e-mail: export@ultratech.com

ÜÇGEN INDUSTRIAL
Tel: +90 212 886 71 91 Fax: +90 212 886 71 94
Web: www.tribecafsp.com
e-mail: info@tribecafsp.com, taskin@tribecafsp.com

ÜÇSAN PLASTİK KALIP SANAYİ
Tel: +90 212 746 63 00 PBX. EXT NO: 115 Fax: +90 212 746 63 11
Web: www.ucsan.com.tr
e-mail: export@ucsan.com.tr

VARIŞ ISI SİSTEMLERİ
Tel: +90 362 266 53 22 Fax: +90 362 266 61 43
Web: www.varisltd.com.tr, e-mail: varissatis@varisltd.com.tr

VENTEKS DIŞ TİCARET LTD. ŞTİ.
Tel: +90 212 659 26 05 Fax: +90 212 659 26 08
Web: www.venteks.com.tr, e-mail: venteks@superonline.com

VIP OTEL EKİPMANLARI
Tel: +90 212 494 50 00 Fax: +90 212 494 50 03
Web: www.vipotelekp.com.tr
e-mail: info@vipotelekipmanlari.com

**VM BAKALİT METAL PLASTİK
MAKİNE İTH. İHR. SAN. VE TİC. LTD. ŞTI.**
Tel: +90 344 236 24 24 Fax: +90 344 236 65 33
Web: www.vmbakalit.com, e-mail: veli@vmbakalit.com

WOODMARKT
Tel: +90 212 670 50 50 Fax: +90 212 670 50 00
Web: http://www.woodmarkt.com, e-mail: info@woodmarkt.com

YAŞAR TİCARET ENDÜSTRİYEL
Tel: +90 312 213 27 62 Fax: +90 312 213 00 35
Web: www.yasarticaret.com, e-mail: info@yasarticaret.com

YENİ SÜPER GAZ SAN.
Tel: +90 212 295 23 42 Fax: +90 212 295 23 43
Web: www.yenisupergaz.com, e-mail: info@yenisupergaz.com

YEŞİLLER/ Açelya, Serbas
Tel: +90 212 659 39 61 Fax: +90 212 659 39 60
Web: www.yesillerplastik.com, e-mail: info@yesillerplastik.com

YEŞİLTAN TURİZM VE MADENİ EŞYA
Tel: +90 212 746 56 56 Fax: +90 212 746 64 23
Web: www.yms.com.tr, e-mail: yesiltan@yesiltan.com.tr

YETKİN MFG. IMPORT&EXPORT INDUSTR
Tel: +90 212 671 22 46 Fax: +90 212 671 22 45
Web: www.yetkincelik.com, e-mail: info@yetkincelik.com

YILMAZ ATATEPE YILMAZ PLASTIC INC.
Tel: +90 212 564 51 00 03 Fax: +90 212 615 41 97
Web: www.yılmazplastic.com, e-mail: info@yılmazplastic.com

YILMAZ FIRÇA SAN. TİC. A.Ş.
Tel: +90 224 243 11 98 Fax: +90 224 243 16 36
Web: www.yfs.com.tr, e-mail: yfs@yfs.com.tr

YİBER ENGINEERING
Tel: +90 216 361 27 77 Fax: +90 216 361 25 26
Web: www.yiber.com, e-mail: info@yiber.com.tr

YNS DAY. TÜK. MAL. TİC. SAN.
Tel: +90 352 321 13 57 Fax: +90 352 321 13 59
Web: www.emerald.com, e-mail: izzet@emerald.com

YONCA LINES MUTFAK
Tel: +90 344 236 30 30 Fax: +90 344 236 46 24
Web: www.yoncametal.com
e-mail: info@yoncametal.com

YÖM-PLAST PLASTİK SANAYİ
Tel: +90 212 875 83 28 Fax: +90 212 875 83 31
Web: www.yomplast.com, e-mail: info@yomplast.com

ZAMBAK PLASTİK SAN.
Tel: +90 212 659 41 15 Fax: +90 212 659 42 90
Web: www.zambakplastik.com.tr, e-mail: export@zambakplastik.com.tr

ZİLAN DIŞ TİC. LTD.ŞTİ
Tel: +90 212 632 23 23 Fax: +90 212 589 63 28
Web: www.zilangroup.com, e-mail: info@zilangroup.com

ZÜMRÜT ART OF GLASS
Tel: +90 258 276 54 30 Fax: +90 258 276 54 99
Web: www.zumrutartofglass.com
e-mail: info@zumrutcam.com

Copyright © 2016 IMMIB All rights reserved. No part of this magazine may be reproduced or used in any manner without the express written permission of the publisher except for the use of brief quotations in a book review.

This magazine may be ordered through booksellers or by contacting

iBooExport
"Reach the World "

Istanbul Office	London Office
EGS Business Park	3rd Floor
B2 Blok No: 12 D.01	86-90 Paul Street
Yesilkoy, Bakirkoy,	London
İstanbul 34149	EC2A 4NE
Turkey	United Kingdom
t: +90 850 460 1 064	t: +44 20 3828 7097

info@ibooexport.com II www.ibooexport.com

ISBN

978-1-947144-70-5 (sc)
978-1-947144-71-2 (e)

We care about the environment. This paper used in this publication is both acid-free and totally chlorine-free (TCF). It meets the minimum requirements of ANSI/NISO z39.48-1992 (r 1997)

Printed in the USA

I006507S

ce

* 9 7 8 1 9 4 7 1 4 4 7 0 5 *